The Oxford Book of
BIBLE
STORIES

The Oxford Book of
BIBLE
STORIES

Retold from the Old Testament by
Berlie Doherty

Illustrated by Jason Cockcroft

OXFORD
UNIVERSITY PRESS

OXFORD

UNIVERSITY PRESS

Great Clarendon Street, Oxford OX2 6DP

Oxford University Press is a department of the University of Oxford.
It furthers the University's objective of excellence in research,
scholarship, and education by publishing worldwide in

Oxford   New York

Auckland   Cape Town   Dar es Salaam   Hong Kong   Karachi
Kuala Lumpur   Madrid   Melbourne   Mexico City   Nairobi
New Delhi   Shanghai   Taipei   Toronto

With offices in

Argentina   Austria   Brazil   Chile   Czech Republic   France   Greece
Guatemala   Hungary   Italy   Japan   Poland   Portugal   Singapore
South Korea   Switzerland   Thailand   Turkey   Ukraine   Vietnam

Oxford is a registered trade mark of Oxford University Press
in the UK and in certain other countries

British Library Cataloguing in Publication Data available

ISBN: 978-0-19-278214-4

10 9 8 7 6 5 4 3 2 1

Printed in China

You can find out more about Berlie Doherty by visting www.berliedoherty.com

For the pupils at Upton Hall School,
past, present, and future.
B.D.

Contents

Introduction
Page 10

The Creation
Page 12

Eden
Page 14

Cain and Abel
Page 21

Noah
Page 27

The Tower of Babel
Page 34

Abraham, Father of All Nations
Page 37

The Cities of Sin
Page 41

Sarai and Hagar
Page 44

Abraham and Isaac
Page 51

Jacob and Esau
Page 54

Laban the Trickster
Page 63

The Journey Home
Page 70

Joseph the Dream-Reader
Page 74

Moses, the Child of the River
Page 88

Moses and the Pharaoh
Page 93

Parting the Waves
Page 104

A Land of Milk and Honey
Page 115

Joshua
Page 120

Gideon Against the Midianites
Page 125

Jephtha's Daughter
Page 130

Samson, the Strongest Man in the World
Page 136

Ruth
Page 146

Samuel
Page 155

Saul
Page 158

David the Giant-Killer
Page 161

David the Outlaw
Page 168

David the King
Page 176

The City of David
Page 180

Bathsheba
Page 185

David and Absolom
Page 188

Solomon the Wise King
Page 191

King Solomon's Temple
Page 197

Rehoboam the Foolish King
Page 200

Elijah the Prophet
Page 202

Elijah in the Wilderness
Page 210

Elisha and the Leper
Page 217

Jezebel
Page 225

Daniel and Nebuchadnezzar
Page 228

Balshazzar's Banquet
Page 235

Daniel and the Lions
Page 238

Esther, the Queen of Persia
Page 243

Jerusalem Rises Again
Page 253

Jonah and the Monster Fish
Page 255

Index of People and Places
Page 262

Introduction

When I was a child, in a small seaside town, I used to go to the beach and listen to a man telling stories. One was about a baby whose mother hid him from the soldiers in the bulrushes, and whose sister Miriam watched and waited to see what would happen to him. Another was about Jonah, who was swallowed by a whale and was later spat out, still alive! Another was about Daniel, who spent the night in a lions' den, and not a hair of his head was touched. While he was talkng, the man stuck little cut-out felt lions, whales, babies, and suchlike on to a felt board; sometimes they would drop off—the desert camel, which turned up in most stories, had a particular habit of doing that. The children would giggle and whistle, but I used to sit with my heart stopped while the story-teller groped in the sand, desperate for him to carry on with his story.

I loved those stories. I didn't even know that they came from the Bible.

Some years ago, Oxford University Press invited me to retell stories from the Old Testament. Imagine my joy at revisiting these stories from my childhood.

In my research I discovered more that I only half knew, or had never met before, and realized that they are all part of one big, important story, like chapters in a book. These chapter-stories are full of danger and treachery, of heroes and villains, of fierce love and simple devotion, of hopeless despair and glorious triumph. I am haunted by characters such as Ruth, stranded in a strange land; Jephtha's daughter, who knows she will never grow up; Hagar, sheltering her dying son from the desert heat; David, shepherd boy, giant-slayer, King . . . Oh—I can't stop there! But they are all in these pages, for you to discover.

I hope you love reading them as much as I loved listening to the man on the beach. Instead of his felt figures, you have Jason Cockcroft's superb illustrations. I hope the stories will stay with you for the rest of your lives.

Thank you to my editor, Vic Tebbs, for her generous and thorough support, and for making sure that my versions of the stories remained faithful to the original text.

The Creation

It is said that

At first there was nothing but God.
Everything around God was chaos
like a wild, wide,
deep, vast ocean.
God filled it with light
and called it Day
and then He called the darkness Night.
That was the dawn and the dusk of the first day.

He divided the oceans into heaven and earth.
That was the dawn and the dusk of the second day.

He created dry land between the earth's oceans.
He made grass and trees and flowers.
That was the dawn and the dusk of the third day.

He made the sun and the moon and the planets and the stars.
He made the seasons that divide the years,
He made the minutes and seconds that divide the hours.
That was the dawn and the dusk of the fourth day.

He made the whales of the sea, the birds of the air,
the creatures of the land.
He made everything that breathes and moves, and he loved them all.
That was the dawn and the dusk of the fifth day.

He made Man.
Man was greater than all the creatures that God made,
all the stars and the fishes and the beasts.
He made man out of the dust of the ground, and he made
woman out of man's own side.
When God breathed life into them, he breathed part of himself.
So man was like him.
Man was in charge of the whole world.
That was the dawn and the dusk of the sixth day.

Now God had made everything that he wanted to make.
Now he could rest.
The last day was blessed,
it was holy and special.
That was the dawn and the dusk of the seventh day.

And it is said that this is how the world began.

Eden

There was once a beautiful garden. It was more full of colour and scent and light than anything we can imagine. Animals wandered about freely, and they were at peace with one another. The lion played with the lamb, and finches flew with hawks. A great river flowed through the garden, watering the flowers that grew on its banks, sending ripples of golden light up the barks of the great trees. It was called the Garden of Eden, and it was made for the first man and woman, Adam and his wife Eve. One day it would be home for all the people that God created.

That was the plan, but the plan went wrong.

Also in the garden was a serpent. He wasn't a man, and he wasn't a beast. He was an angel when the world was first created, but because he was too proud God had thrown him out of Heaven. Once, before Adam and his wife were made, he was God's favourite. Now he was angry that God had rejected him, and he came to the Garden of Eden to seek his revenge. He had red eyes that gleamed like garnet stones, and white wings that shimmered when the sun or the moon was on them. He had more freedom than anything else in the garden, and he was clever and crafty. He could do anything he wanted to do, and go wherever he chose to go. But he chose to follow Adam and his wife, like a beautiful, colourful, silent shadow. He watched everything they did, and he was jealous because God loved them.

In the dusky evenings, when the sun was going down and filling the garden with amber light, God used to walk in the garden with Adam and

Eve and show them everything he had made for them. The red-eyed serpent followed them, and watched, and listened.

In the middle of the Garden of Eden there were two trees. One was the tree of life itself. Its roots were deeper than the earth, and its branches climbed towards the sky like hands reaching up to heaven. The other tree, the most beautiful tree, was the tree of knowledge of good and evil. Every branch hung with fruits that were round and ripe and bursting with juices. When they came to this one God always stopped and turned to look at Adam and Eve.

You must never eat the fruit from this tree, he warned them. *If you disobey me, I will punish you.*

They held hands and promised they would never touch the tree. Why would they ever do anything to disobey God? they asked.

I tell you, you must never eat the fruit of this tree, God said. *Or you'll have pain, and fear, and you will die.*

Adam and Eve smiled. What were these words, pain and fear, and what did it mean, to die? God smiled back at them, but it was a sorrowful smile. And the red-eyed serpent smiled too, dark in the shadows.

Adam and Eve passed the tree of knowledge every day when they walked round the garden. They always stopped to admire the fruits that clustered like jewels on its branches; emerald green and amber gold, ruby-red and amethyst-purple, according to their ripeness.

'It's a very beautiful tree,' said Adam, 'but we mustn't touch it.'

'No, we'll never touch it,' Eve agreed. 'We'll just look at it, won't we?'

The red-eyed serpent folded his wings and waited. He curled up under the tree and sipped the juicy fruits as if they were nectar. Then he watched silently until the next time Eve walked on her own.

When she came to the forbidden tree he hummed softly:

'*How sweet* the fruit must be, that dangles from that tree.'

Eve stopped and listened, amazed that a serpent could speak exactly the thoughts that were inside her head. She went up to the tree, close enough to smell the sweet fruit. She could have put out her hand and touched the tree, she was so close, but she remembered what God had said, and she walked away.

Next time Eve walked near the tree, the serpent spread out his gorgeous wings and flew up onto one of the branches.

'As ripe as the sun is the fruit on this tree,' he sang. 'As ready to eat as it will ever be.'

Eve stopped, surprised again to hear a serpent singing words that she could understand. She went up to the tree and held up her hands like a bowl. If one of the fruits had fallen, it would have dropped right into her hands. But she remembered what God had said, and she went away.

Next time she went by the tree the serpent had twined himself around the trunk. His wings were shimmering like the moon on water, and his eyes were as red as setting suns.

'Eat, Eve, taste and eat,' he whispered.

Eve stopped. The serpent's head lay just by one of the fruits.

'Eat, Eve. Just taste. You won't die. It's quite safe.'

She hesitated. The fruit was brimming with juices, ready to burst.

'Eat, Eve, taste and eat. And you will be as wise as God. You will know everything. See how ripe it is, how sweet.'

Eve tilted back her head and put her lips round the fruit, and the juices trickled down her face, down her arms, down her body. She closed her eyes, and the serpent disappeared.

'Eve, Eve, are you mad? What are you doing?'

Eve opened her eyes and saw Adam running towards her. She stared at the half-eaten fruit and plucked it from the tree. 'I just wanted to taste it. Try it, Adam. Just a little bit. It won't do any harm,' she begged him.

'No,' he said. 'We promised God we wouldn't touch this fruit.' He took her hand and tried to lead her away from the tree, but she held out the fruit to him.

'Just one bite. It's so sweet, you'll love it.'

He shook his head. 'Come away. Drop it, please.'

'Adam, if we eat this fruit we'll know everything that God knows. This is the Tree of Knowledge.' She held out the fruit again. 'Taste, Adam. Taste and eat with me. It's safe. We won't die.'

And Adam took the fruit, and ate it, and the juices trickled down his body like wine.

'Now you know everything,' laughed the serpent, twisting himself out of the shadows and twining round the tree like tendrils of ivy. 'Everything. Pain, fear, and death. Death, and fear, and pain.' His laughter echoed round the Garden of Eden.

'What have we done?' gasped Adam.

'What will God say?' Eve moaned.

It was evening. The birds came home to roost in the branches of the tree. The sun was sinking fast, fast, and they knew that soon God would be coming to walk and talk with them. They looked at each other in despair.

'What shall we do?' they asked each other.

'Fear, and pain, and death,' the serpent sang.

Adam and Eve realized that they were as naked as the animals. Desperate with fear and shame, they ran and tried to hide themselves. They pulled leaves down from fig trees and tried to cover their bodies with them.

But there was no hiding from God. He came straight to them. His shadow fell like night across them where they crouched, their heads in their hands. He stood in silence, looking down at them, and they knew that he had seen them eating the forbidden fruit. He knew everything.

Why have you covered yourselves with leaves? he asked them sadly.

Why are you ashamed of your nakedness now,

when you have always walked freely and unashamed?

Take these furs, and cover yourselves, if you must.

They scrambled into the clothes that he handed them. They stood in front of him like frightened children, afraid of what he might do.

Now tell me. Have you eaten fruit from the forbidden tree?

Adam pointed at Eve and said, 'It was her fault. She gave me the fruit, and I ate it.'

Why?

'The serpent tricked me,' Eve whispered. 'He made me do it.'

You disobeyed me, God said.

I gave you everything, and you disobeyed me.

I loved you, and yet you disobeyed me.

He turned away from them as if he couldn't bear to look at them any longer. The serpent was dangling from the tree, laughing, and God roared at him in anger.

You!

You will never live as you please again.

You will never walk with men

or fly with angels.

You will slide on the ground on your belly,

and you will eat the dust of the earth.

You are a snake, and men will always despise you.

The serpent slithered down from the tree. The feathers dropped from his wings and drifted away like leaves. An oily, papery skin crinkled across his body. The red of his eyes faded like a quenched fire. His forked tongue flickered, in, out, in, out, and he slid through the long grass, hissing. Adam and Eve shrank away from him.

Then God turned back to Adam and Eve. *Go away from me.*
You are banished from my garden.

'What shall we do?' Adam asked him, shaking with fear.

Now you are afraid! God said.

Outside this garden you will toil and sweat

from the rising of the sun to the rising of the moon.

Your limbs will ache with toil

your bellies will hurt with hunger,

and still you will work.

Eve will bring children into the world

through pain and blood and labour.

And at the end of it all, you will die.

You came from dust,

you will return to dust.

Fear, and pain, and death.

Now go! he shouted. *Go.*

Adam and Eve ran, clutching their clothes around themselves, crying
and stumbling out of the Garden of Eden. The grass turned to thorns
and thistles and dragged at their skin, their feet bled on the sharp stones,
the sun grew cold and the sky wept down on them. Everywhere around
them was bare, stony, gritty soil.

When they turned to look back to where the garden had been they
saw an angel with the face of a lion, brandishing a sword of fire. A tongue
of flame whipped this way and that: it was impossible to go back into the
garden. The heat of the flames drove them further and further away, on
and on, until they could run no more.

Then they stopped. The fiery angel had gone; the voice of God had
gone. Adam and Eve felt they were alone in a strange, harsh world. They
knew that they would never see the beautiful garden again.

Cain and Abel

Adam and Eve's first two children were boys, Cain and Abel. Cain chose to be a farmer. The ground was stony and sandy and it was difficult to make things grow, but the family depended on him to bring grains home for bread, and lentils and barley for stews. In the summer the sun beat down on him as he worked, and in the winter the winds tossed the sand in his face and scratched his eyes.

Adam told him that when the harvest was ready he must put the best of it on a stone for God, and bring the rest for the family to eat.

'Why do I have to do that?' Cain asked.

'You must,' Adam said.

'But why? I've worked so hard for every grain I've grown. Why do I have to give the best of it away?'

'Because God says so.' Adam looked across the mean fields that Cain had dug and sown, and at the plants that struggled to live there. 'Remember, God is everywhere; in the sand and the sea and the sky, in the stars and the sun. He sees everything, and he knows everything. He knows everything that you do. When your harvest is ready, and you give the best to God and bring the rest home for us to eat, I will be very proud of you,' he said.

The younger boy, Abel, chose to be a shepherd. He spent all day looking after his animals, protecting them from the wolves and lions that ranged in the distant mountains. He understood the hills and the patterns of the weather. He could read the stars and know exactly where he was. Sometimes he could be away from home for weeks on end, following the pastures, taking his sheep and goats to the good grazing grounds.

When his animals were ready for eating he brought them home again. His parents heard him singing as he came over the hill, and rushed out to welcome him. There would be a good meal that night. One of the lambs would be prepared for Eve to roast over the fire. But first of all, the fattest and tenderest lamb would be prepared, not for the family, but for God himself. Abel placed the lamb on the stone and prayed that God would accept this gift in thanks for his safe return. Instantly, a tongue of fire licked down from the sky and engulfed the stone, and when it died out, the lamb had gone.

'God liked your gift,' Adam said, kissing his son. 'Now we can all eat.'

'Cain hasn't made his offering yet,' Abel pointed out.

Cain put a bundle of lentils and barley on the stone. It hadn't been a good harvest, and he didn't take the trouble to sort out the best from the worst. There didn't seem to be much point. Cain's offering lay on the stone, untouched. God spoke quietly to him:

There is a beast inside you, Cain.

Sin is lurking like a wolf at the door to your heart.

Don't let it in.

I am waiting for your good offering.

Then I will be pleased with you.

But Cain did nothing, and still his offering lay untouched. Adam saw what had happened, and said nothing. After a while Cain gathered up the rest of his harvest and took the baskets in to Eve.

A cooking fire was lit for the evening meal. Night comes fast in the desert, and soon the sky was full of stars. Sparks flew like smaller stars from the bonfire, and the air was filled with the sweet smell of woodsmoke and the juices of the roasting meat. When the meal was ready the family sat round the fire to eat, and the light of the flames was golden on their faces and in their eyes as they listened in wonder to Abel's stories.

'Cain,' said Eve, 'did you make your sacrifice?'

Cain nodded. He threw a heavy log on to the fire, making the flames squat down like desert rats with red eyes.

'I didn't see God's flame come down to the stone.'

'I told you. I made my sacrifice,' said Cain. 'I gave oats and barley and lentils from my fields.'

'Perhaps they weren't good enough for God,' Adam said. 'I am ashamed of you, Cain.'

Cain said nothing.

'Have more meat,' Abel said. Cain tore meat from the roasted lamb but his hunger had left him. The meat was tasteless now. He stared at his brother, who was laughing and singing with his father. For the first time in his life Cain was jealous of Abel, and the jealousy was like the white heart of the fire, eating into him, spreading through his bones and his blood.

Next day he went out to his fields early, full of a black temper that snarled like a beast in his heart.

'Come and join me, Abel,' he shouted. 'I want to show you something.'

As he waited for his brother he turned the sandy earth over, rough in his fury, and God spoke to him. He tried not to listen, but the voice was loud and strong in his head.

Why are you so angry, Cain? If you want to please me, you know what you have to do.

Cain tried to drive the voice away. All he could think of was Abel's laughing face in the firelight, his eyes bright, his voice singing, happy because he had sacrificed his best beast and God had accepted it. It must mean that God loved Abel best. He had left Cain's sacrifice withering on the stone. His father had seen it there and had said nothing to him, but then in front of the whole family he had shown that he was ashamed of what Cain had done. Now Adam loved Abel best, too.

Cain went back to the stone and kicked away the sacrifice he had left there. He could hear his brother singing as he washed himself in the river, and then calling his flock round him. Cain followed him at a distance. Soon Abel would be crossing the fields on his way to the pastureland on the far slopes of the mountain. He would not be back home again till the moon had filled out and waned again, and he would have his fat lamb or kid ready for sacrifice; a new welcoming, a new homecoming. Cain went closer, silent and quick, watching.

At last Abel looked up, sensing his presence. 'You made father unhappy last night,' he said. 'I was sorry about that.'

The quick fire of jealousy flared up in Cain's heart. 'What has that to do with you? I never want to see your face again,' he shouted. He picked up a stone and jumped on his brother, taking him by surprise. Abel had no time to struggle. Cain pounded him and pounded him with the stone until he was dead.

Cain stood up, all his anger spent. Abel was lying still and silent on his own shadow. Then the shadow began to creep away from him, and Cain could see that it was not a shadow at all but blood, soaking into the soil. Panicking, he scrabbled into the soil with his bare hands. The earth fell back into the hole. He picked up the stone that he had used to murder his brother and drove it into the ground again and again, flinging the soil behind him, and when the hole was deep enough he rolled Abel's body into it and heaped the earth back. The dark blood seeped through it. He was frantic with fear. Adam would see, Eve would see. They would find Abel's body on Cain's field and they would know he had murdered him. He piled earth high around the body and ran for home, and when he turned round, the black shadow of blood was oozing through the mound.

It was still there the next day, and all the crops around it had wilted, and still the shadow spread. Cain gazed around him in despair as his crops drooped their heads.

Cain, said the voice of God. *Where is your brother?*

'How do I know?' Cain shouted, angry and afraid. 'Am I my brother's keeper?' He knelt down and trickled the thin soil through his fingers. 'He's not a baby. He can look after himself.' He pulled the dead plants out of the soil. The black shadow trickled around him.

The blood of your brother cries from the earth, God said.

Is this your sacrifice to me?

'No,' said Cain, covering his face with his hands, hiding himself from God. 'Look, my crops are dead! They're ruined!'

Your crops will always die, said God sadly.

The stain of your brother's blood will poison your fields
for ever.

'What can I do?'

You must leave this place.

There is no home for you here now.

Go out into the wilderness.

Cain gazed at the empty expanse of desert stretching out in front of him. 'Don't send me away,' he begged. 'I don't know how to live out there. I'll die.'

You will find your way.

I will protect you.

Cain felt a nudge on his forehead as if a hand had stroked him. He touched it, and felt that the flesh there was raised like a star.

Men will see this sign on your face, God said.

They will know that you are Cain.

They will know that you must be left alone.

No one will harm you.

'Where will I go?'

You must walk in the path of the setting sun.

You have lost your home, Cain.

Your people will always wander,

nomads in the desert.

Now go, and find peace.

Cain felt a storm rising round him in a mist of sand. The voice of God had left him. He turned to look back towards his home, and in the distance he could see Adam and Eve, his mother and father, bending to their work. He lifted his hand, and then the storm-mist thickened and they disappeared from sight. He felt alone on the earth.

Noah

One day, God decided to destroy the world.

He did it because he was angry. The descendants of Adam and Eve had travelled and spread, they had built fine cities and they had learned to look after themselves and each other. But after a time they began to fight among themselves and with the animals and birds; they became cruel and violent. They did not love one another, and they did not love God. Yet he had made them, he had made men and birds and beasts, fishes, insects, and worms. He made them all, and now he was so angry that he wanted to destroy them all.

I am sorry I made you, he roared, and his mighty voice thundered around the mountains and rolled over the valleys.

The people laughed, and God's fury swept like a wild wind across the earth. Only one man heard him. His name was Noah, and he was six hundred years old.

God saw that he was good, and decided to spare him.

Noah and his family were working in the fields, gathering corn, far away from the clamour of the cities, and Noah heard the anger of the wind and knew it was the voice of God.

'Listen,' Noah said. 'God is going to destroy the world. Every man and bird and beast, everything that lives and breathes.' He drew his wife to him. 'Nothing will be left. Nothing.'

They held each other and cried. 'It's because of our wickedness,' his wife said. 'No wonder God's angry, when there's such wickedness in his world.'

When God saw them weeping he knew that Noah and his family were good people, and that they understood his sorrow as well as his anger. He saw how they looked after each other and loved one another as a family should, and he decided to spare them, just them.

Noah, he said, and the old man heard him and bowed his head.

I will destroy the world,

everything that moves and breathes,

except for you and your wife, your sons and their wives.

Listen.

This is what I want you to do.

Noah closed his eyes so he would remember every detail of God's instructions.

That evening he called his sons together. 'We have to build an ark,' he said. 'A kind of house without foundations. A kind of boat.' His voice was trembling as he tried to explain what was in his mind's eye. He crouched down and drew it in the sand with a sharp stick. 'It must be made of cypress wood and painted with black tar, so it will float.'

'A house that floats!' Shem laughed. 'What do we need that for?'

'That's what we have to do. It must have three decks with many stalls inside each one. And it must have a roof over it. It must have a door at the side, there. And at the top, it must have a window.'

'But what are all the stalls for?' asked Japheth.

'That's the strangest thing of all,' Noah said. He knelt back on his feet, and spoke slowly, remembering the words in his head. 'We're going to live in this ark for a long time, and we're to take two of every creature with us. Two of every creature that moves and breathes on the earth and flies in the air. That's what the stalls are for. It's stranger than a dream, but that's what we have to do.'

Ham puzzled over the shape of the ark that Noah had drawn. 'How big will it have to be?'

'I know exactly,' Noah said, straightening up. 'Three hundred cubits long.' He walked slowly away from them, counting aloud for three hundred steps. 'And fifty cubits wide!' he shouted.

'Huge!' said Japheth. 'We'll have to pull all our barns down to build this, and fell the trees. How high will it be, if it has three floors?'

'Thirty cubits,' said Noah.

'That's eight men, one on top of the other.' Shem climbed on Noah's shoulders. 'Come on, Ham! You stand on my shoulders now, then Japheth gets on yours, and we'll have half the height of the ark.'

Japheth gave his brother a leg up, and Shem pulled his arms, but Ham never managed to climb up the wobbling Noah on to Shem's shoulders. After three attempts they collapsed in a heap on the ground, and their wives ran to see what all the laughing was about. Noah stood up slowly, brushing sand from his hair and his beard.

'Now we know what we have to do,' he said. 'And when it is done, the world will be destroyed.'

And they all went silent, and thought about the horror and mystery of the destruction of the whole world.

They started building the ark immediately, the whole family helping. They pulled down all their barns and felled all the cypress trees in the area. As the strange flat-bottomed ship began to take shape, passing herdsmen came to watch and to jeer at the old farmer building a boat in a field that was miles from the sea.

'God is going to flood the world,' Noah told them. 'Maybe if you change your ways he will save you, too.' But his words fell on deaf ears. They told him he was mad.

When the ark was ready they painted it with tar so every seam and crack was filled and no water could leak in. Then they divided the three storeys into dozens of stalls and filled them with straw so the animals would be comfortable there. It took months to gather the animals together from the forests and mountains, and they kept them in folds and pens while they were waiting. They carried in barrels of grain, figs and dates, apples and lentils, corn and bread, honey and cheeses, and stored them in the cool, dark hold of the ark.

Then Noah drew back the big door and the women drove in the animals, some that they might need for food, and two each of every creature that moved and breathed; the tigers and leopards, the horses and cows, the rats and the weasels, the moths and the eagles, the ants and the worms; two of every kind. It was amazing to see, and it was terrible to hear. Piglets had to be torn from their sows, baby monkeys clung to their mothers and screamed in fright and had to be wrenched away. The mother elephants roared and grieved when their babies were taken from them.

'No,' Noah said to his wife. 'You can't take more than two of each.'

Everything was ready. Noah and his wife took a last, sorrowing look at the world that they were leaving, and followed their family into the ark. They pulled the heavy door shut behind them and sat in the darkness, waiting.

And at that moment God released the rain. It lashed down from the sky and surged up from under the earth. In minutes the rivers had burst their banks and came streaming across the fields. Waterfalls cascaded down the sides of the mountains, sweeping away trees as if they were blades of grass, sweeping away rocks like grains of sand. People climbed onto the roofs of their houses and screamed for mercy, and the walls crumpled beneath them like paper. They swam to the ark, beating their arms uselessly against its sides. 'Help us, help us. We're drowning! Take my baby, just my baby. Take my old mother. Take me, save me!'

I will destroy you all! I will destroy the whole world with my rain, God roared.

As the water rose, the ark was lifted from the ground and began to float. Noah and his family could feel the sea swaying beneath the floor of the ark. They clung to each other in the darkness, hearing the rain lashing like whips across the roof, hearing the cries of people screaming for help. Still it rained, and every creature drowned, and every man and every woman and every child drowned. Still it rained, and the birds of the air could fly no higher and fell exhausted into the water, and still God's anger surged and boiled, and still the rain pounded down. The world was destroyed, just as God had said it would be.

Then after forty days God breathed gently, and the rain stopped.

Everything was silent.

'Is it safe to look outside?' Noah's wife asked.

'Not yet,' said Noah. 'We must be patient.'

After many more weeks the ark touched rock at the summit of a mountain called Ararat, and came to rest. They knew then that the anger of God was over. The flood waters began to subside. At last they went up to the top deck and pushed back the shutters of the little window. A white mist swirled round the ark. Gradually it began to clear, and above them they could see that the sky was blue and that the sun was full and bright.

'I never thought I'd see the sun again!' Noah's wife laughed. She held out her arms, and the warmth was like a blessing on her skin. The rest of the family crowded round to see this wonderful thing; a sky without rain, and the sea stretching for miles around them.

Noah picked out one of the ravens and held it up to the window.

'Tell us if there is land anywhere,' he said, and let the raven go. Its wings gleamed blue-black in the sun as it soared away from them. Below it, the sea rippled like a shoal of silver herrings. The raven flew high and low, looking for dry land, and as it flew the waters seeped away down the sides of the mountain.

But the raven did not return. Noah sent out a dove: 'Tell us if there is land anywhere.' She couldn't fly as far as the raven and there was no place yet for her to perch. Her wings grew weary and she returned to the ark.

A week later Noah sent out the dove again. 'Tell us if there is land anywhere.' And that evening she returned with a sprig from an olive branch in her beak.

'Things are growing,' Noah said, full of happiness. 'The world has begun again.'

They pulled back the great door of the ark and the animals streamed out and ran and crawled and flew in every direction, each in their pairs, to make their nests and lairs again, to bring up their young. Noah and his family made their way down the side of the mountain, marvelling at the warmth of the sun and the freshness of the grass and flowers. As soon as they reached the green valley they built an altar and made a sacrifice to God for sparing them. They were safe, but they were afraid, because they knew what God could do.

I promise you that I will never drown the world again, God said to Noah and his sons.

I will never destroy the world again.

Noah,

you are the father of the new world.

Your children will have many children.

They will be the new people.

Night will follow day,

summer will follow winter,

harvest will follow seed time.

That is how it will be in the new world.

You will see by my sign that this is a promise to you.

The family of Noah fell on their knees to thank him, and when they looked up they saw that the sky was flooded with the colour of every creature and every flower, an arc of light that seemed to touch the earth and to touch heaven.

And that is the story of Noah, who lived for nine hundred and fifty years, and from whose children all the nations of the world were born.

The Tower of Babel

After the flood, God waited to see what would happen next. Noah's sons and their wives had children, and they all had children, and so did they. They lived together in harmony, in a place called Babylon, all speaking the same language, and they were one huge family. They understood each other because they were so alike. They decided that they would all like to live together and they organized themselves into work gangs to build a huge house that would be like a city. The walls would be made of bricks baked in the sun, and it would have many storeys. It would be bigger than anything that had ever been built, a massive ziggurat reaching right up to the sky.

This was to be the last time that anything like this happened, where men and women worked together without squabbling, without hatred or jealousy. They all wanted the same thing, to live together in a tower that reached up to heaven. 'Everyone will see our magnificent home,' they said. 'And they'll know what a great people we are.' They puffed themselves up with pride at the thought of it.

Teams of brick makers and joiners, builders and decorators worked side by side, marvelling at the beauty of the great tower of Babel that they were creating. And when it was finished, they flocked inside, laughing and singing and chattering, all those families of Noah happy because they were going to live together in the wonderful tower.

But God looked down on them and said,

This is not the way it should be.

You have become too vain and proud.
What will you try to do next,
now you have built a tower that touches the sky?

So he breathed on them, and in the middle of speaking to each other they saw looks of puzzlement and surprise on each other's faces. Nobody could understand what anyone else was saying any more. The more they shouted and waved their arms, the less they understood. Now they were stamping and yelling, glaring at each other, pointing and poking and jabbering wildly to try to make themselves understood. They were angry and confused and frightened, and the noise of all the different languages was so terrible that at last they covered up their ears and ran out of the tower. They all ran off in different directions, clinging to their children and loved ones. They travelled all over the world to be as far away from their old home as possible, and there they settled.

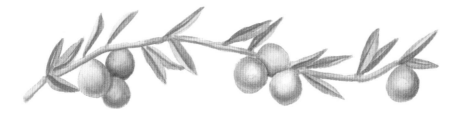

Abraham, Father of All Nations

Noah's son Shem became the father of the Semite people, and one of his descendants was a man called Abram. He was asked to make the greatest sacrifice a man can make.

Abram was very rich, and he lived with his wife Sarai and his nephew Lot in a beautiful house in Haran. You would think he had everything he wanted in the world, but he didn't. In his heart Abram longed for a son, and when you long for something so much, it is all you can think about, day and night, waking and sleeping. His wife Sarai was barren, but he never gave up wishing for a child. The time came when Sarai was too old to have children, and still Abram's heart ached for the child he would never have.

One day the voice of God sang to him, and the song was wonderful and strange.

Leave your home, and leave your land,
cross the desert to the place that I will show you.
There your children will grow and multiply,
And you will be the father of the greatest nation of all time,
I will bless you and make your name famous
I will bless those who love you
I will curse those who hate you
All the people of the earth will be blessed because of you.

Abram repeated the words of the song to Sarai, and she listened in amazement.

'This is impossible,' Sarai insisted. 'We're too old to travel across the desert. It will take years of hardship. We don't know how to live like that, like wandering nomads. And we'll never have children, Abram, so how can they grow and multiply?'

But the mysterious words sang again in Abram's blood and bones, and he knew he must obey, and that it must be possible because God had said so.

'We must go, all the same. We must learn to live under the stars,' he said.

So they closed up their fine house in Haran, rolled a few possessions up in rugs to tie on the backs of the mules and camels, and set off with their slaves and servants and animals. Abram's nephew Lot and his wife and daughters went with them. They all slept in goatskin tents, which they had to tether to boulders to keep from blowing away in sand storms. They had never known such discomfort before. They had to trudge from place to place in search of food for their animals in the dry desert scrub, just like the poor tribes of the desert. Whenever the sparse grass was eaten they had to roll up their tents, load up their camels, and move on, weary and hungry, month after month after month. They had no food because there was famine in the land. At last, desperate, they came to the land of Egypt. It was rich and fertile along the banks of the Nile; the cities were beautiful, and the people were prosperous.

'We could stay here,' Sarai said. 'We could be wealthy and comfortable again. Please, Abram. This would be such a fine place to live.'

Abram knew that they were still a long way from the land that God had chosen for them, but he was old and tired and, like Sarai, he wanted to stay still, to stop wandering, to eat well and to sleep away from the wind and the cold desert nights. So he agreed to stay. And very soon he realized that the pharaoh had fallen in love with Sarai, and he thought of a plan that would help them all.

'Pharaoh will ask you to marry him,' he said. 'Don't refuse, and don't tell him you're married already. Pretend I'm your brother, not your husband, or he'll kill me. Marry him, and we'll have more wealth than we've ever had.'

So that is what Sarai did. She and Abram lived as brother and sister in Pharaoh's palace. They feasted and slept in great luxury, and you would think it brought them complete happiness. But Abram had a deep sadness inside him. He did not have what he wanted most in the world: a son.

And God was angry because they were not doing what he had asked them to do. He put a terrible curse on every woman in Pharaoh's court. He made them all barren like Sarai, like empty wells, like dry deserts, every single one of them. There would be no more children, ever, in the grand court. Pharaoh's line would die out, and his great household would die with him.

'There must be a reason for this curse,' Pharaoh insisted. 'I've done nothing wrong.'

He called together all the slaves and servants that Abram and Sarai had brought with them, and ordered them to tell him everything they knew about this brother and sister. When he discovered the truth he drove them out of the palace, out of the city, out of his sight, and they were left to wander again; lonely and afraid in the heat and dust of the great desert.

Abram was a wealthy man by now, with plenty of livestock, but the food in the desert was so poor that the animals began to starve and Lot's herders and Abram's herders squabbled among themselves.

'All our beasts are trying to eat the same miserable patch of grass,' Lot complained.

'We mustn't quarrel about this,' Abram said. 'Look how much land there is around us. You choose where you want to live, and we'll go the other way. That way there'll be plenty for all of us.'

'I choose the valley,' Lot said, without a moment's hesitation. 'It's as rich and fertile as Egypt.'

And so the two families parted company, and Lot led his wife and daughters down to the rich pastureland of Jordan, near the towns of Sodom and Gomorrah, and there they pitched their tents. And, for a time, they were happy.

The Cities of Sin

It's not very often that angels come to visit you, but that is exactly what happened to Lot.

Lot and his family soon found that they needed to keep themselves to themselves. The ways of the people of Sodom and Gomorrah were not their ways. During the day they were kind and friendly, but at night they changed. Perhaps they drank too much of the wine that the plentiful vineyards produced; it went to their heads and made them crude and boastful. They had no sense of dignity or shame. They brawled in the streets at night, out of control, and respected nobody. It was not safe to be outdoors. At times like that Lot kept his wife and daughters in the house and his door locked.

One quiet evening Lot was sitting outside the gates of Sodom, enjoying the coolness that comes before sundown, when he saw the two angels coming towards him. There was no doubt that they were angels; they didn't walk like ordinary men, and there was a radiance about them that was even brighter and more beautiful than the setting sun. Lot went down on his knees to greet them, and invited them to come to his house.

'Thank you for your kindness, but we have come to see what Sodom is like,' the angels said. 'We intend to walk round the streets and perhaps spend the night in the square.'

But Lot wouldn't hear of it. 'It isn't safe here at night,' he said. 'It's no place for strangers. Please do me the honour of staying in my house. At this very moment supper is being prepared, and you will be most welcome to share it with us.'

So the angels agreed, and Lot took them home and introduced them to his family. They were made as comfortable and welcome as any visitors would have been. Where Lot's family came from, strangers were honoured guests. But before long all the brawling men of Sodom and neighbouring Gomorrah were banging on Lot's door and shouting for the visitors to come out to them.

Quietly Lot went out and shut the door behind him. He tried to reason with them, but they charged at him, almost crushing him against the wall of his house. One of the angels opened the door and pulled him back to safety, just in time. The other angel cast a spell of blindness on the mob, and they groped about in the frightening darkness, bellowing with fear.

'You must leave this town,' the angels told Lot. 'God has heard how evil the people here are. He sent us to find out just how bad it is, and now we have seen it for ourselves and he will want to punish them. He will destroy Sodom and Gomorrah as soon as daylight comes. But we want you to be spared.'

Lot called his wife and daughters and told them what the angels had said. 'They want us to leave now, straight away,' he whispered urgently.

'But this is our home,' his wife said. 'We like it here.'

'Can't we just stay in our house?' Lot asked.

'Believe what we tell you, and go, as quickly as you can,' the angels said. 'We promise you will be spared. God talked to Abram in the desert about this.'

'Abram?' Lot was astonished to hear his old uncle's name mentioned.

'He asked God to spare Sodom and Gomorrah if we found ten good men living here, and God agreed. But we have not found ten good men, we have only found one. The cities will not be spared, but you will if you leave at once. Go now, go now.'

Still Lot hesitated, and the angels grabbed his hands and pulled him away from his house and out through the gates of Sodom, and his wife and daughters ran after him, full of fear because they had no idea what was going to happen. When the angels let go of Lot's hands they told him to run as fast as he could, as far as he could.

'And whatever you do, don't look back. You must never look back, any of you.'

Instantly the sky went dark and livid; the earth heaved like a writhing beast. Terrified now, Lot and his wife and daughters lifted the hems of their robes and ran for their lives. The earth was grumbling and bellowing, fire gushed up to the sky and down from the sky, thick stinking yellow smoke belched round them, so bitter and salty that they could hardly breathe. On they ran, choking and spluttering and gasping while the tongues of flame and acrid sulphurous smoke spluttered after them; on they hurried, up the mountain to safety.

And there Lot's wife paused for a moment. She thought of the town they had made their home, she thought of her house, and her garden of fig trees and flowers. She turned to look at it for one last time.

And she never turned back, and she never breathed again.

She was turned into a pillar of salt, and there she stands to this very day on the ridge of Mount Sodom. Far below her lie the ruined cities of Sodom and Gomorrah, the cities of sin, and long ago they were washed over by the bitter waters of the Dead Sea. The valley is the lowest point on earth, and nothing grows there, nothing lives there, and the shores are crusted with crystals of salt, that are as white as bones.

Sarai and Hagar

When Lot had gone, God spoke to Abram again and told him what he must do.

Look East, look South,
look West, look North
these lands are for you and your children
and your children will be more plentiful than the grains of dust that lie upon
the ground.
Walk upon the land I have given you, Abram.

So Abram walked on with his household until he came to the oaks of Mamre, and there he built an altar to God. But Sarai was not happy.

'Why do we have to do this?' she cried. 'We're old and homeless. Time is passing, Abram, and we still have no child, and never will. We've nothing to live for now.'

'Except God's promise,' Abram reminded her, and she laughed bitterly.

'All that was a long time ago,' she said. 'How can we go on like this?'

Abram was close to despair. He went out of the tent alone and walked into the night. The desert was huge around him, like a vast, dark sea. And in the great emptiness of the night God came to him in a vision and spoke to him again.

Do not be afraid.
Look up at the stars, Abram. Can you count them?

Abram gazed up at the shimmering sky. 'No. There are too many.'

You will have many children,
and they will have many children,
and from them will come as many people
as there are stars in the sky.
You will be the father of the greatest nation on earth.

Abram shook his head. 'My wife is barren. Besides, she's too old to have children.'

I tell you, one day you will have a son,
and this land that I give to you
will be the land of your son and of all his people.

Abram flung himself to the ground, and the sand whispered and sifted against his face and his hands. 'How?' he asked. 'How?'

But God was silent, and the stillness of the night then was so deep that Abram lay wide awake, in awe of the great mystery of God's words to him.

When Abram told Sarai that God had spoken to him in the night, she was troubled too.

'How can you be the father of a great nation?' she asked. 'You have no son. I'm too old to give you a child. It's impossible.'

Then she looked at Hagar, the slave girl who was so close to her that she thought of her almost as a younger sister, and she knew what she could do.

'Hagar is young enough to give you a child,' she said. 'She's my slave. She can do it for me.' The idea was a good one, and she knew it, but all the same it made her sad. More than anything else in the world, she wanted to be able to give Abram a son herself. But she called Hagar from the women's tent, and gave her to her husband Abram.

Soon Hagar became pregnant. Sarai was bitterly jealous, but she tried to keep her feelings to herself. After all, she owned Hagar, and she would own Hagar's child when it was born. She treated Hagar so badly that the girl ran away into the desert to get away from her taunts.

'What have I done?' Sarai whispered to herself, out of her mind with shame. 'Without Hagar, Abram will never have a child.'

But it was too late for sorrow. Hagar had gone.

Hagar trudged through the desert, deeply afraid. She had no idea where to go, or how she could look after herself, alone in this wilderness of sand, without animals or shelter.

'Please help me,' she prayed. 'Please let my baby be born safely.'

That night when she lay under the black sky she saw a glittering light coming towards her, and knew that she was not alone. The voice of an angel breathed across her.

God has heard you. Go back to Sarai. You will be forgiven. You will have a son, and his name will be Ishmael, and he will found a great nation.

So Hagar went back to Sarai. The old woman cried with relief to see her again. She knew that her slave could have died out there in the desert, with Abram's child inside her. And soon afterwards the baby boy, Ishmael, was born. Instead of being a slave like Hagar, Ishmael was taken into Sarai and Abram's tent as their son. Abram was filled with joy.

'I have a son at last!' he laughed. 'God's promise is fulfilled, Sarai. I am eighty-seven years old, and all these years I have waited and prayed, and now God has granted my wish. God is good to us, Sarai. We can be happy now.'

Sarai nodded and smiled, but all the same it grieved her to see her slave taking the baby Ishmael in her arms and suckling him. 'God has been good,' she agreed sadly. 'I'm happy for you, Abram.' She was more unhappy than ever. God's promise was a wonderful thing, but Hagar was the mother of Abram's son, not Sarai. She could never forget that.

And then, when Ishmael was thirteen years old and Abram was a very old man of ninety-nine, God appeared to him again.

This is my covenant, my promise to you.
From now on your name will be Abraham,
which means, father of many nations.
I will give you the land of Canaan
for you
and all your offspring.
And your wife shall be called Sarah.
She will give you a son.
The children of her children will be kings.

One day Abraham, as he came to be called, was sitting in the shade of his tent by the oaks of Mamre. He saw three men appearing out of the mist of a desert storm like figures in a dream. But these were not ordinary men. They did not walk like ordinary men. It was as if their feet did not touch the ground. And the glow about them was more dazzling than sunlight. Abraham shielded his eyes as he watched them approaching.

'Are these angels?' he wondered. 'Make food for them, Sarah. Roast the best meats we have.'

He went to greet the men, and invited them to rest and shelter from the storm. Sarah was in the women's tent helping to prepare the food when she overheard Abraham calling Ishmael to come and meet the strangers.

'This is my son,' he said.

Sarah could hear the pride in his voice. She turned her head sideways, hiding her eyes so the women would not see how the old sadness and jealousy flared up in her again. Then she heard one of the strangers say something that made her laugh out loud.

Sarah will give you a child.

'Fine thing!' Sarah called. 'I'm nearly a hundred years old, stranger!'

The stranger came into the tent where she was preparing food and looked down at her quietly.

Even so, what I tell you is true.

Sarah's laughter turned to trembling. She went on her knees, filled with wonder. She realized then that the stranger who was speaking to her was God himself.

And at last the greatest marvel that could be imagined came true. Sarah and Abraham had a son of their own. His name was Isaac, after the Hebrew word for laughter. Abraham was happier now than any man in the world, and you would think that Sarah would have been happy too. She had a child at last. But there was one thing that spoiled her happiness, and that was Ishmael. She wished he had never been born. She knew her feelings were wrong, but she couldn't help it. She had given Abraham the son he wanted. She wanted Isaac to be his only son.

Her jealousy grew like a fire inside her; and at last it was so great that she couldn't bear to see Hagar or Ishmael any longer. She ordered the slave girl and her son to leave them and go and live in the desert, and this time she told them they must never, ever come back. Abraham was deeply distressed when he found out what Sarah was doing, but God promised him that Ishmael, too, would father a great nation one day. Abraham gave Hagar food and water so they wouldn't starve, and let them go.

But before long the food and water ran out. Hagar had no means of shelter, nowhere to hide, nowhere to go. The sand was blisteringly hot under her feet, and the sun poured down relentlessly. She and her child soon became weak with hunger and thirst. When Ishmael grew too feeble to walk Hagar carried him in her arms as if he was a baby again, and when she grew too weak to carry him she left him in the tiny pocket of shade under a shrub and crawled away to die. She couldn't bear to listen to him begging for water; she crawled further away till she couldn't hear his voice any more, and then she lay down and waited for death.

But the angel of God shimmered round her and Hagar heard a voice sighing like the wind that comes before rain.

Ishmael will live. He will be the father of a great nation.

She opened her eyes and saw a spring of water gushing out of the sand; a magical, wonderful thing. She cupped some in her hands and carried it to Ishmael, and then more, and more, till he had the strength to drink for himself. Then he and Hagar walked to a safe place and found a home there. Many years later, when he grew old enough to marry and have children, Ishmael founded a nation, just as the angel had said.

Abraham and Isaac

So at last Sarah had her wish. She and Abraham and Isaac were a family; there was nothing to take away from Abraham's great love for his child.

Abraham taught Isaac everything he knew. They did everything together; tending the flock, caring for the household. He showed him how to read the stars and the sun and the wind, how to know the plants and animals, where to look for food and water when there seemed to be nothing at all. They were as close as brothers, and Abraham loved him more than he loved himself. Every day he spoke to God and thanked him for the miraculous gift of a son.

And one day, God spoke to Abraham, and the words he spoke turned the old man's blood cold with fear.

Abraham.
Take your beloved son to the land of Moriah
and there on the high mountain
offer him as a sacrifice to me.

It was as if the light of the world had gone out. Abraham remembered the night of despair that he had spent, long ago, when God had spoken to him under the stars. Had he come through all that, had he spent years of hardship in the desert, had his greatest dream been answered, only for this; to be asked to kill his own child? Yet he knew that he must do what God told him. It was not possible to refuse. It was not possible to hide from God.

He said nothing to Sarah. How could he have told her what God had asked him to do? How could he have told her what was in his heart, the grief and despair, the fear and the love? He drove his agony deep inside himself. He simply said that he was going to a place in the distant mountains to make a sacrifice to God, and that he would take Isaac with him.

The mountains were so far away that it took three days to walk there. It was a great adventure for Isaac, but he was aware of his father's silence and he knew that he was deeply troubled about something. When they reached the mountains they left their donkey behind. Isaac carried the branches; Abraham carried the knife and the pot of fire. They climbed to a high crag with a flat boulder like an altar, and it was there that Abraham stopped at last.

'This is where we must make our sacrifice,' he said. 'Put the wood on this stone. It will be our altar.'

Isaac gazed round him. 'We haven't brought anything with us to kill, father. No lambs or kids, no calves. There's nothing here. What are we going to sacrifice?'

'God will provide the lamb for the sacrifice.'

'Where is it?'

The dry wind sent whispering echoes round the crags. Abraham said nothing more, but went on laying bits of wood on the altar stone. In his father's silence, and in the sorrow of his father's eyes, Isaac knew the answer.

His voice trembled with fear and disbelief. 'Am I to be the sacrifice?'

Still Abraham couldn't speak, but could only cover his face with his hands and nod. He put his arms round Isaac, and there was never such love between father and son as there was that day on the mountain.

Then Abraham bound his son and laid him on the altar slab, and lifted his knife to kill him. He had to hold it with both hands because he was shaking so much. The sun flashed on the blade, blinding them both.

Stop, called the voice of God, and it was as if glorious music was pouring out of every rock, every grain of sand. Abraham lowered his hand, and Isaac opened his eyes and sat up.

You have shown how much you love me, Abraham.

Spare your son.

Abraham and Isaac looked round as if they were in a dream. The voice faded away; the mountains were silent. All that could be heard was the bleating of a ram that was caught in a thorn tree. They knew that this ram was to be their sacrifice.

Before they left the mountain, Abraham went down on his knees, and God sang to him.

Your children will be
like the stars in heaven,
like the grains of sand in the desert.
You will own land
even where you are a stranger.
Your people will be great,
because you listened to me,
because you obeyed me,
Abraham, Father of all Nations.

Jacob and Esau

Many years later, when he was dying, Abraham passed on to Isaac the traditional blessing from father to son.

'Everything that I own will pass to you, as you are the first-born son. Always remember this blessing, my son.'

'I will,' Isaac promised.

'And before you die, pass the blessing on to your own first son.'

'I will.'

The next thing Abraham did was to send his servant to Mesopotamia in search of a wife for Isaac. Although they were settled in Canaan, he wanted his son to marry a girl from his homeland. Then he felt he could rest in peace.

When the servant arrived he was tired and very thirsty after his long journey. He saw a young girl standing by a well and asked her for something to drink. She gave him water for himself and his camels, and offered him shelter in her father's house.

'Who is your father?' the servant asked.

'My father is Bethuel, the son of Nahor,' the girl replied.

'I'm delighted to hear that,' the servant said. It meant that he had already found Isaac's future wife, because Nahor was Abraham's brother.

The girl's name was Rebeka. Soon after the marriage she told Isaac that she was going to have a baby. But this was no ordinary child. It struggled so much in her womb and gave her such pain that she wished she were dead. But God spoke to her in her agony and told her a strange thing:

Two nations are in your womb.

One will be stronger than the other,

and the younger will master the older.

It was not easy to give birth to the fighting twins. The first to be born was Esau, but his brother Jacob was born almost at the same moment, hanging on to Esau's heel as if he wanted to pull him out of the way and race him into the world.

Although they were twins, they were not at all alike, neither in their appearance nor in their nature. Esau was red-haired; even his hands and his neck were covered in hair as if he was an animal of the wilderness rather than a human child. He grew up to love the wild; he loved to roam, living and sleeping like the animals. He was a hunter, and his father loved him best because he understood the desert well, just as Isaac himself had done.

'One day you will inherit everything I have,' he told Esau. 'And you will receive my blessing as my first-born son. I'm glad that it will come to you.'

Jacob bitterly resented this. He had lost his rights to everything simply because he had failed to pull his brother out of the way at the very moment of birth. Even his name meant 'he who hangs on to another's heel' so he would have to go through life knowing always that he came second; and everyone he met would know this too. He brooded on the unfairness of it, but he kept his resentment to himself. He was much quieter by nature than Esau. He liked to stay near the tents, cooking and herb gathering like the women, instead of wandering away for days and weeks on end and taking his chance with the wild beasts. He was very close to his mother, Rebeka, and she loved him best of her sons because of his gentle nature. She never told him what God had promised her. *The younger will master the older.* How could this be true?

One day Esau returned from hunting while Jacob was preparing a meal for his mother and father. Esau hadn't managed to catch anything for days, and he was weak with hunger. He found Jacob cooking a stew of red lentils that he had picked from the fields.

'I've had no luck hunting,' Esau said. 'Father will be disappointed. He loves nothing more than a roasted deer from the mountains, but I've caught nothing.'

'Then he'll have to make do with what I give him, won't he?' said Jacob. He sprinkled a handful of mint and thyme into the lentils, and the smell rose up, sharp and delicious, making Esau's stomach growl with hunger.

'I'm famished. How about giving me a bowl of that stew, Jacob?'

A bowl of lentil stew was not much, yet at that moment Esau was so hungry that he wanted it more than anything else in the world. Jacob realized that for the first time in his life he was more powerful than his brother, because he had what Esau wanted. He had food, and Esau had nothing. He saw his chance, and grabbed it. He stirred the stew thoughtfully, scooping a little out with a fistful of unleavened bread, savouring the taste. Esau watched him.

'If you want it so much, I'll swap a bowlful for your birthright,' Jacob said. A bowl of stew and a scrap of bread might be nothing at all to him, but a first son's birthright was everything, and he knew that well.

'My birthright doesn't mean anything to me!' Esau laughed. 'What use is it anyway if I'm about to die of hunger? Let me eat, Jacob, and you can have it for all I care.'

'Swear that on oath,' Jacob demanded.

'All right. I solemnly swear that you can have my father's blessing, which is my birthright,' he laughed again. 'Now food, brother, please!'

So Esau ate, and tossed away all his rights, just like that. No wonder

Jacob smiled. And listening in her tent, his mother Rebeka smiled too.

The twins' father, Isaac, was old and blind by this time. One day when he knew he was near to death he called Esau into the tent where he was lying. Rebeka was kneeling by him, cooling his fever with damp cloths.

'I could die at any time now,' Isaac said.

Esau knelt by his father and put his arms round him, embracing him.

'You're a fine huntsman, Esau. Take your bow and arrow and bring me some lovely game from the mountains, so I can enjoy my favourite meal. Then I'll give you the blessing that is your birthright because you're my eldest son. Then I'll be able to die in peace.'

As soon as Esau had gone, Rebeka went to Jacob and told him that Isaac was about to give his final blessing.

'But you must have it, not Esau,' she said. 'Go and fetch two young goats and plenty of herbs, and I'll cook your father one of his favourite meals. Then you can take it to him and receive the blessing of the first-born instead of Esau.'

'But he'll know I'm not Esau!' Jacob laughed. 'Even though he can't see us, he can tell us apart. As soon as he touches me he'll know, because Esau is so hairy and I'm so smooth.'

'I'll see to that,' Rebeka said. 'You do as I say.'

So Jacob did as his mother said. He caught the goats and brought them to her with a bundle of sharp-smelling herbs. In his tent Isaac could smell the wonderful food that was being prepared, and he looked forward to having a last meal with his favourite son before he passed on the blessing.

As soon as the food was ready, Rebeka tied the skins of the goats across Jacob's neck and his arms and hands. 'Remember, you're Esau now,' she said, kissing him. 'Go in to your father.' And she gave him the pot of food and the bread she had baked for Isaac.

'Who's this?' the old man asked when he heard the sound of the tent skin being lifted and footsteps approaching him. It didn't sound like the way Esau walked.

'It's Esau, your first-born,' said Jacob, deepening his voice. 'I've brought your favourite meal, father.'

Isaac frowned. It didn't sound like Esau speaking.

'Come a bit closer.'

Jacob went closer and put the food down. Isaac breathed in deeply as his son bent over him. 'Ah, you smell of the animals of the fields, just like Esau.'

'I *am* Esau. Eat, father,' Jacob said, 'and give me the blessing of the first-born.'

But still the old man did not touch the food.

'How come you caught the wild game so quickly?' he asked. 'No sooner did I ask for it than you bring it in, all prepared and cooked for me.'

'God helped me to find it,' Jacob said quickly. 'Eat, father.'

'Come closer,' Isaac said. 'I want to make sure you're Esau.'

Jacob knelt in front of his father, and Isaac touched the boy's neck and arms, hairy with the goatskins that Rebeka had tied on to him.

'So,' Isaac said. 'You have the voice of Jacob, but you have the skin of Esau. Are you Esau or Jacob?'

'I am Esau,' said Jacob. 'I am your first-born son.'

Isaac nodded and was satisfied. He ate the food and drank the wine that Jacob had brought for him, and then he held out his arms. 'Come for your blessing, Esau.'

Jacob went to his father and kissed him.

'I give you the blessing of the first-born,' Isaac said. 'May God bring rain to your crops and ripen your harvest of grain and vine and beast. May people serve you, for you are their master. May nations bow down to you, for you will be powerful. Hatred be on those who hate you, and love be on those who love you. That is the blessing that I give to you, my first-born son.'

Not long afterwards, Esau came back from hunting. He had caught some fine game, and he set to at once to prepare and cook it in the way his father liked best. The old man was asleep when Esau went into the tent, but the sound of footsteps on the sand startled him.

'Who's this?' he asked.

Esau went straight up to him and set the food down in front of him. 'It's Esau, with the meal you asked me for. You've not had to wait too long for it, father.'

Isaac knew at once that this was truly his eldest son, and he realized that Jacob had played an awful trick on them both. Tears filled his milky, sightless eyes.

'Come here, come here, my favourite son,' he said. 'Let me embrace you, for I have no blessing to give you. Jacob has stolen it by pretending to be you.'

'But bless me too, father. Surely you can bless me too!'

'No,' the old man shook his head. 'The blessing has been given.'

'But bless me, father. Bless me too!' Esau clung to the old man and they wept together.

'The blessing cannot be undone, nor can it be given twice,' Isaac said.

'Have you only one blessing? Don't die without giving me your blessing.'

'I have already made Jacob your master. What more can I do for you? This is all I can say,' the old man sighed. 'Your home will be on poor land. Little rain will come to water your crops. You will live by the sword, and in time to come you will be able to free yourself of your brother's power over you. That is the best I can say to you, my son, my beloved Esau.'

'In time to come!' Esau repeated bitterly to himself. 'How long will that be? Must I serve my brother all my life? I hate him. Even though he is my twin brother, I hate him with all my heart.'

As soon as Isaac had died and the time of mourning was over, Esau planned his revenge on Jacob. I'll kill him, he thought. That way I'll win back the blessing that he stole from me.

He watched Jacob's every movement, and when the moon was full he sharpened his knife, ready. The time had come.

But Rebeka saw what he was doing and recognized the murderous anger in Esau's heart, and she guessed what he had in his mind. She ran to Jacob and roused him from his sleep.

'Run!' she whispered. 'Get away as fast as you can, and as far as you can, or your brother will kill you.' When he hesitated, she hugged him to her. 'I don't want you to go. Do you really think I want to lose you? Of course I don't. But I want to save your life. Go, do as I say, go and find yourself a wife. Go to my brother, Laban, in Haran. He'll help you. And when it's safe, I'll send for you to come home.'

So Jacob set off, alone, as soon as dawn came. He was not used to the life of a wanderer, he didn't understand the sun or the stars, and he was

afraid. When it was dark he lay down on the sand with a stone under his head for a pillow. And during that night he had the most wonderful and frightening dream. He dreamt that he saw a ladder coming down from the sky, gleaming with an unearthly light, and he had a sense of angels with quivering wings moving up and down the steps that led from earth to heaven. At the top of the ladder stood one who was more radiant than any of them, more brilliant than the sun. His voice sounded across the night, and was terrifying to hear.

I am the Lord, the father of Abraham and Isaac.

The land where you lie

belongs to you and to your children.

They will spread like the dust of the earth

to the north, to the south, to the east and to the west.

I am with you now, Jacob.

I will be with you at all times.

Jacob started out of his dream in terror, knowing that he had heard the voice of God. He made a pillar of the stone he had been resting his head on, and poured oil on it, because he knew that this was a sacred place. Now he knew what he had won when he had stolen Esau's birthright and blessing. It would never leave him now, this gift and burden of power.

'God is with me now. He will feed me and clothe me.' He took up his bundle of belongings, ready now to move on. 'One day, one day, I will return in peace to the home of my father.'

Laban the Trickster

Jacob won his brother's birthright by trickery, but many more tricks were to be played on him and by him before he had a chance to meet Esau again. It began on the day he fell in love.

He arrived in Haran in the middle of the day, and approached a group of shepherds who were standing round a well. He knew about animals, and he thought it was high time for them to be out on the pasture, feeding, but when he said this to the shepherds they told him that they were waiting for all the flocks to gather so that the well would be opened for them to be watered at the same time.

'Rachel hasn't arrived yet,' they said. 'When she comes with her flock, we can open the well.'

'I'll sit with you a while, and drink when the well is opened,' Jacob said. He settled down on the ground with the shepherds, sheltering under a tree from the high sun. 'I've come here to find my mother's brother,' he told them. 'Do you know him? His name is Laban.'

'We know him well,' they answered. 'In fact, this girl that we're waiting for is his daughter.'

Jacob's heart grew weak for a moment. Perhaps Rachel was the cousin his mother wanted him to marry. He didn't know if he was ready to meet her yet, but one of the men called, 'Here she is at last.'

Jacob turned to see a girl leading her flock of sheep to the well. She was very beautiful, and he fell in love with her at once. He ran to help her to roll away the stone that covered the well, and when she turned to him to thank him, he leaned forward and kissed her impulsively, and then cried, because he couldn't believe that he had found his future wife so easily, and that she could be so beautiful.

'I am your cousin,' he told her. 'I've come all the way from Canaan to see you.' He didn't tell her why, even though he was already sure that he was in love with her.

'Come home with me and meet my father,' she said. 'I'm sure he'll be pleased to meet you.'

Laban greeted Jacob courteously and welcomed him into the house. 'Stay with us as long as you like,' he told him. 'You're one of us now, Jacob.'

That night Rachel and her older sister, Leah, helped their mother to prepare food for him. Jacob watched the girls chopping herbs while he talked to Laban. Leah has beautiful eyes, he thought, but Rachel is lovely. Everything about her is lovely. No wonder I fell in love with her at once!

He told Laban about the death of Isaac, and that he and his twin brother Esau were now enemies. 'It's no longer possible for me to live at home,' he told him. 'My life is in danger because of what I did. My mother sent me to you for help.'

'She did right,' Laban told him. 'You're one of us now, Jacob. You're my flesh and blood.'

They embraced, but still Jacob didn't tell Laban his real reason for coming to his house. 'You're very kind,' he said. 'And in return, I'll help you as much as I can, just as I used to help my parents. I don't know much, but I'm a good farmer.'

He made himself useful, and took on the handling of Laban's flock of sheep and goats, which he could see were good stock. One day, perhaps, some of them would be his. At the end of the first month Laban came out to the pasture where the animals were grazing and stood watching how Jacob handled the animals.

'I'm very pleased that you've shown so much willingness to serve me and help me, but you really should have a wage for this,' he said. 'What can I give you?'

Jacob's eyes wandered over to where Rachel was sitting by the flock of young lambs, and he smiled at her. She smiled across at him.

'I want to marry your daughter,' he said.

'Nothing would please me more,' Laban began, then he saw that Jacob was looking at Rachel. But she was his youngest daughter, and it was the custom for the oldest girl to be married first. Still, he was a clever man, and he didn't want to lose Jacob. He would find a way round that.

'If you work for me for seven years, you can marry her,' he said. That would give Leah plenty of time to find a husband, and it would keep this useful nephew working for him.

'Gladly,' Jacob said.

Well, seven years passed like seven weeks, because Jacob was so happy at the thought of marrying his beautiful Rachel. By the time the wedding feast drew near, however, Leah was still unmarried. She looked sourly at her father and said, 'Do something! I will be disgraced if Rachel marries before I do.'

'Don't worry,' Laban smiled, putting a comforting arm round her. 'I've thought of that.'

So the wedding went ahead. Jacob was happier than he had ever been before. He kept looking at his bride in her long veil and thinking, at last, after all these years, Rachel is mine. But Laban had other ideas about that.

Before the wedding feast was over, Jacob took his wife's hand and led her to the darkness of their room. And it wasn't until the next morning that he discovered the truth: that it wasn't Rachel who was lying in his arms, but Leah.

He stormed out to Laban. 'You've tricked me!' he said. 'How could you do this to me?'

Laban spread out his hands in a gesture of helplessness. 'What else could I do?' he asked. 'You know the laws of this country. The oldest daughter must marry first. But now you have married Leah, you can also marry Rachel,' he promised. 'Stay with Leah as her husband for the rest of the wedding week, and when all the guests have gone home, you can have Rachel as well.'

'Two wives!' laughed Jacob. 'Well, that sounds a good bargain.'

'But you must work for me for seven more years,' sly Laban added. 'Seven years for each daughter. That's my price.'

So Jacob agreed, and worked for Laban for seven more years, and thought nothing of it. You would think that all four of them would be happy with this arrangement. But they weren't. Leah was very unhappy because Jacob couldn't bring himself to love her. And Rachel, the loved one, found that she couldn't give Jacob the children they both longed for. But Leah was fertile, and one after another she gave Jacob sons: Reuben, Simeon, Levi, Judah. She was poorly loved, she was poor in beauty, but she was rich in her fertility, at least for the moment.

In despair Rachel said to Jacob, 'Please let me give you sons too!'

He was icy-cold with her. 'Who do you think I am,' he said. 'God?'

'Then my maid can be a surrogate mother,' she said. 'Take her instead of me. Take Bilhah as a wife, and her children will be mine and yours.'

So Bilhah the maid gave birth to Dan and Naphthali. Leah, eager as ever to please Jacob, gave him *her* own maid as a surrogate mother too. This maid was Zilpah, and she gave birth to Gad and Asher. Then, Leah gave birth to two more sons, Isaachar, and Zebulun, and, at last, a daughter, Dinah. If she had ever been jealous of her sister, she could smile in triumph now. Between her and her maid, she had given Jacob eight sons and a daughter.

And then, when all seemed lost for poor Rachel, a miracle happened. She became pregnant. She gave birth to a son, and his name was Joseph, and he became the most famous of all Jacob's sons, and the most loved.

All this happened while Jacob was still serving Laban. At the end of the seven years he looked at his wives and his twelve children and said, 'It's time for me to go home now.' He asked Laban to release him and to let him travel back to his own country.

'No man can have worked harder for a master,' he said.

'I agree,' said Laban. 'Name your wages and I will give them.'

'Gladly. I would like livestock. Let me sort out your cattle and sheep and goats today—let the pure coloured ones be yours, and any that are spotted or striped or speckled, let me take.'

And this is where the trickery began again, because although he agreed to Jacob's idea, Laban went quickly to his flock and withdrew all the speckled goats and the spotted cows and the stripy sheep and hid them, so all that were left were pure coloured ones.

But Jacob knew a way of overcoming Laban's trickery by even more magical trickery of his own. Where Laban's pure cattle and sheep and goats came to drink, at the very well where he had first met Rachel and kissed her so tenderly and hopefully, there he placed some branches of almond trees. He peeled away bits of bark so the white flesh showed through in speckles and stripes and spots. Next time these animals bred, they produced young that were speckled and spotted and striped, and these were the ones that Jacob claimed as his own.

He herded them all together, proud that at last he had the finest flock of animals that he had ever seen, finer than Laban's own. He called his wives and children together and told them to load up their camels with what was theirs, because they were leaving at once without saying goodbye to Laban.

But a trickster father has a trickster daughter. Before they left, Rachel crept into Laban's tent and stole all his golden idols and gods and hid them under her camel's saddle. She didn't tell Jacob she had done this. They left in the middle of the night, not saying goodbye to Laban, not even telling him they were leaving.

As soon as Laban discovered that he had been robbed he chased them for seven days. In a dream God told him that he must do nothing to harm Jacob, but still he pursued him over plains and mountains, shouting with fury. He caught up with them in the hills of Gilead.

'You have carried away my daughters as captives, you have stolen my household gods!' he screamed. 'And now you steal away without saying goodbye.'

'I'm no thief,' said Jacob calmly. 'I have never done anything dishonest to you, Laban, whatever you might have done to me. I served you for seven years and seven years for my wives. I served you for six years for my animals. And I would not touch your false gods and idols—they are nothing to me, why should I steal them? Search our baggage if you want.

You won't find anything of yours.'

Laban's men did so but found nothing.

'Forgive me if I don't get down to embrace you, father,' said Rachel, sitting high up on her camel with her father's idols under her saddle. 'It's the wrong time of the month for me, and I'm not well.'

'I've been tricked,' Laban groaned. He wanted revenge, but he was helpless to do anything, because of his dream. 'These are my daughters, my grandchildren, my animals,' he insisted. 'All your riches have come from me.'

'What is to be done then?' Jacob asked.

'Let us make a pact, Jacob.'

'I agree. I am tired of wrangling with you. I'm tired of the way you have treated me. I want to be left alone with my wives and my children and everything I have worked for. Most of all, I want to go home.' He closed his eyes, wondering now if his mother would still be alive, and what had happened to Esau. Would he ever be welcome again in his own home?

'We will build a cairn of stones,' he said. 'And that will mark the boundary between us. I will never cross that boundary in your direction, and you will never cross the boundary in my direction. That way, we will never trouble each other again.'

So the cairn was built by Laban's and Jacob's sons. They made a sacrifice there and ate a meal, and then, after kissing and blessing his daughters and grandchildren, Laban went his way, and Jacob went his.

And the golden idols? Well, they were still snug and warm under Rachel's saddle.

The Journey Home

And far away in Edom, Esau lived as he had always done, roaming the hills, hunting, living off the land and using his wits and his sword to keep himself alive. He was at peace with the winds and the stars and the mountains. He had no idea that Jacob had become a very wealthy man. Twenty years had passed since he had last seen him.

If Esau had been an eagle of the mountains he would have seen his brother's long caravan of camels travelling slowly to Canaan. He would have seen Jacob riding proudly in the lead, and his two wives Leah and Rachel, riding behind him in their fine clothes, with jewels on their fingers and dangling from their ears; nose-rings and bracelets sparkling. He would have seen the eleven sons and the daughter, the large household of servants and slaves. He would have seen the brindled, spotted, and speckled cattle, goats, and sheep, driven along by their shepherds. The long line of brightly covered camels stretched across the desert, signalling Jacob's return. The dust of their travelling rose up into the motionless sky, and Esau knew nothing of it.

He was preparing a goat over a scrub fire when a stranger rode towards him, breathless and dusty, calling out to him that he was searching for a man called Esau.

'Why? Who wants him?' Esau asked cautiously.

'My master does,' the messenger said.

'And who is your master?'

'Jacob.'

Esau's hand rested on his sword. 'Jacob is my brother,' he said. 'What is his message?'

'He has sent me to tell you that he is coming home.'

Some days later, the same man returned to where Jacob and all his household had set up camp. He had a message from Esau, the brother who had been cheated of everything, and the message was this:

'Tell Jacob that I am bringing four hundred soldiers to meet him.'

Nothing more.

Even as the words were spoken, Jacob could hear, far away, the sound of hundreds of horses pounding across the sand, and he was deeply afraid.

'They are coming to kill me,' he said. 'And my wives and children. My brother will take my wealth away from me.'

Jacob divided up his household into two halves and told them to travel separately. That way, even if Esau destroyed half of them, the other half would be saved. Then he fell on his knees and begged God to save him.

'You said you would stay with me at all times,' Jacob said. 'But here is my brother's army coming to kill my wives and my children. You said I would have as many children as there are grains of sand on the shore, yet my brother is coming to kill us all. Please save me!'

God was silent.

So Jacob sent Esau presents of cows, sheep, goats, oxen, drove after drove of them, in the hope that his brother would accept the gifts and forgive him for what he had done. Still the four hundred horsemen advanced. Jacob feared that he was about to lose everything he owned in the world. When he crossed into the red-cliffed valley of Jabbok, he sent his wives and children and servants away for safety.

He was alone, watching and waiting in the darkness. Suddenly a man in black, a stranger, appeared from nowhere and wrestled with him as Jacob had wrestled with his brother Esau in their mother's womb. All night long they fought in the sand, neither winning, neither losing, each as strong as the other, each as weak as the other, until the man struck Jacob so fiercely on the side that he put his hip out of joint.

Let me go, the stranger said at last. *Dawn is coming, I must go.*

'I must have your blessing first,' Jacob said.

Tell me your name, the stranger said.

'Jacob.'

You have fought against man, and you have fought against God. And you have not lost. From now on, you will be called Israel.

'Tell me *your* name,' Jacob begged, but there was no reply, and when he struggled to his feet the stranger had gone. All Jacob's guilt and his shame and his fear had gone with him because he knew he had seen God.

Now in the light of day he could see the four hundred soldiers of Esau coming towards him and he knew what he must do. He must face his brother at last. He ran across the ford so he was ahead of Rachel and Leah and all their children, ran on into the morning to meet Esau, and bowed to him seven times.

Esau dismounted from his horse. The words of his father's blessing sang to him: *You will live by the sword, and in time to come you will be able to free yourself of your brother's power over you.*

The two brothers held out their arms to each other. 'Why have you brought so many animals and servants with you?' Esau laughed.

'They're for you. Please accept them, Esau.'

'I am blessed,' Esau replied. 'I already have everything I need in life, and now I am doubly blessed because my brother has come home. Welcome to you and your family.'

Esau and Jacob hugged and kissed each other and wept with joy, and at last their feud was over.

Joseph the Dream-Reader

Of all his sons, Jacob loved Joseph and little Benjamin best, because their mother was his favourite wife, Rachel. To show how much he loved Joseph, he gave him a wonderful coat with long flowing sleeves, dyed with the rich blue of pomegranate.

'Look at Joseph, parading round like a king!' Simeon said. 'Goatskin cloaks aren't good enough for him, it seems. I'm sure the sheep are going to be impressed!'

The other brothers laughed. All of them, except the youngest child of all, Benjamin, were united in their jealousy of Joseph. Rachel had died when she gave birth to Benjamin, and the two boys were very close to each other. But the ten older brothers thought Joseph was a show-off, with his peacock cloak and his angelic good looks. They also thought he was strange. He had a mysterious gift, which they did not understand. He could read dreams.

'I had a peculiar dream last night,' Joseph told his brothers one day. 'Do you want to hear it?'

'I expect you'll tell us anyway,' Judah said.

'It was a strange dream, but I think you'll understand it. I dreamed we were all in the field, binding sheaves of corn. Mine grew up straight and tall and strong. And yours all bowed down to mine. You know what that means, don't you?'

The brothers all turned away from him.

'It isn't my fault,' Joseph said. 'I can't help my dreams!'

'You could keep quiet about them,' Judah suggested.

But Joseph couldn't keep his dreams to himself. They were so powerful and strange and wonderful, he had to share them.

'I had another dream,' Joseph told his whole family one evening. They were gathered round the fire under the stars; it was a time for storytelling, a time for sharing dreams. 'I dreamed that eleven stars fell out of the sky and bowed down to me, and then the moon, and then the sun. They all bowed down to me.'

'King Joseph!' little Benjamin laughed.

'I know! And you were all my servants! Even my father and his wife . . . !'

'No more dreams!' his father interrupted angrily. 'We don't want to hear any more of this talk, Joseph.'

The ten older brothers exchanged glances, pleased to hear the favourite son being chastised. They hated him all the more. They wished he had never been born, and that was the truth.

One day they were working together some way from home and they saw Joseph in his gorgeous coat coming towards them across the flat, windy plain.

'Here's the dream-reader!' Reuben said. 'I'd like to give him some nightmares. That would shut him up!'

'Never mind nightmares. Kill him!' Gad suggested. 'Dig a pit and chuck his body down it.'

'Then we'll see how good his dreams are!' Simeon laughed.

They set to digging the pit, laughing about how they would choose to kill him.

'No, don't kill him,' Reuben said, realizing that they were serious. 'We can't do that. He's our own flesh—do we want his blood on our hands?'

'Then we'll tie him up and throw him naked down the pit,' Simeon said. 'And let him rot in the sun, and let the vultures peck at him.'

So as soon as Joseph reached his brothers they tore his famous coat from him. They bound his hands and feet and flung him down the pit. Reuben was anxious about this, so he went away, planning to come back at the end of the day and rescue Joseph. He would have been punished enough for his boasting by then. The others sat round the pit, eating the bread and olives Joseph had brought for them, ignoring his screams of anguish.

Before they had finished their meal, they were approached by a group of traders from the people of Ishmael in Arabia. Their camels were stacked with cinnamon, balm, and myrrh to sell in faraway Egypt. Judah stood up, shielding his eyes from the sun. He had a new plan now.

'Want to buy a slave?' he called.

The horsemen stopped, and the brothers hauled Joseph out of the pit.

He glared at them defiantly.

'We'll take him,' the leader of the traders said. 'He looks a strong and spirited lad.'

He tossed twenty silver pieces down to the brothers, and they grovelled in the sand for them while Joseph was led away. The brothers couldn't believe their luck. Now they would never have to bother about him again.

When evening came Reuben returned to look down the pit. He saw that it was empty and tore his clothes in sorrow. 'The boy has gone! What are we going to do?' he shouted to his brothers.

Between them they smeared Joseph's gorgeous coat with blood from a baby goat, and hurried home to tell Jacob that his favourite son had been torn to pieces by a mountain lion.

But when they told him, they turned away and hid their silver pieces, and they covered their faces in shame, because it seemed that their old father would die of sorrow.

Joseph trudged for miles alongside the ambling camels, while the sun beat down on him and the hot sand burned the soles of his feet. When they reached Egypt one of the traders threw him a goatskin to cover up his nakedness, and he was led through the gates of a huge city to the slave market. He had never been away from the desert before, and now the noise and bustle of the streets, the clatter of carriage wheels, the jostling throngs of people in their strange, bright clothes and peculiar wavy hair bewildered him. They jabbered at him in a strange language that he didn't understand. The other captives stood with their heads bowed down, but Joseph stared back at the people who poked him and prodded him as if he was no more than an animal.

At last a quiet, dignified man called Potiphar, an officer in Pharaoh's court, came in search of a slave. He liked the proud way Joseph held himself, and bought him at once. He had Joseph brought to his house and given good, clean linen to wear, and instead of making him labour in the fields he gave him household duties. As soon as Joseph began to pick up the language of the Egyptians, Potiphar made him his personal servant.

Joseph became everyone's favourite because he was strong and willing and clever. There was a special quality about him that made him different and mysterious; it was the quality he had been born with, when God made him a reader of dreams. He was also very good-looking. The Egyptians found him fascinating. He became an important member of Potiphar's household, and before long Potiphar's wife fell in love with him. She was quite shameless. She dressed herself in her finest gowns and put perfume in her hair; she rubbed sweet oils into her skin to make herself irresistible, and she flirted with him publicly. She tried to kiss him when he was near her, tried to stroke his cheeks; she would never leave him alone.

'Don't you love me, Joseph?' she murmured, teasing and tempting him with her seductive smiles, trying to draw him into her bedchamber.

'No, how can I love you? You're Potiphar's wife!' Joseph said. 'We shouldn't be alone together like this.'

She was so angry at his rejections that she wrenched at his tunic and screamed that he was trying to attack her. Guards dragged him to Potiphar, who ordered him to be thrown into prison, and there he would have spent the rest of his life, if he hadn't been a reader of dreams.

This is how it happened.

Among the other men in the prison were two of Pharaoh's servants; one was his wine servant and the other was his baker.

'I had a strange dream last night,' the wine servant said one morning.

'I saw a vine with three branches, and as I watched, it budded and blossomed and then bore fruit. I gathered the grapes in and pressed them into wine for Pharaoh.'

'I can explain your dream,' Joseph said. 'The three branches are three days. Within three days Pharaoh will forgive you and you will be serving him again.'

'Good!' the wine servant marvelled. 'But is this true?'

'Of course it is. I know how to read dreams. And remember me, won't you, when you're a free man? Tell Pharaoh I've done nothing wrong, but they've left me in here to die.'

'Explain my dream now,' the baker said. 'I dreamt I had three baskets on my head, full of things I'd baked for Pharaoh. And a flock of birds landed in the top basket and ate the lot. What do you make of that, dream-reader?'

Joseph looked at him sadly. 'In three days Pharaoh will have you hanged, and birds will come down and eat your head.'

'That's not so good,' said the baker. 'Surely it isn't true?'

But it happened just as Joseph had said; within three days the wine servant was released, and the baker was hanged.

The wine servant forgot all about his promise to Joseph for two whole years, until Pharaoh himself began to have strange dreams. He was so troubled by them that he sent for all the magicians and wise men of Egypt to explain them to him, but nobody could.

'These dreams are sending me mad!' he said. 'Can't anybody help me?'

It was then that the wine servant remembered Joseph. 'I know a dream-reader,' he said. 'He's a Hebrew in one of your prisons, but he hasn't done anything wrong. And he can certainly read dreams. He told me my dream meant that you would release me, and you did. And he told the baker that his dream meant that he would be hanged, and that happened, too.'

Joseph was sent for immediately. He washed himself and was given clean linen to wear, and he went to the gleaming palace. All the courtiers stood around, and the priests and magicians, all eager to hear what he would say. He bowed down to the great ruler.

'I hear you can read dreams,' Pharaoh said.

'I can tell you what God means by your dreams,' Joseph replied. There was a hush in the court. No magician had ever claimed to speak with God before.

'I have two dreams,' Pharaoh said. 'They come back night after night to haunt me and wreck my sleep. In the first, I am standing by the banks of the great Nile, and seven cows come out of the water. They are fat, healthy beasts. Then seven skinny cows rise out of the river and eat the fat ones.'

'Go on,' said Joseph. 'Tell me the second dream.'

'It's just as strange. I see seven ears of rich, ripe corn, all on one stalk. Then I see seven thin ears, blasted by the east wind, thin and ragged. And these seven thin ears of corn eat up the ripe ones.'

Joseph nodded. 'Both dreams mean the same thing. Soon there will be seven years of plenty, followed by seven years of famine. You must store the harvest of those seven good years in the granaries, ration it so plenty is saved, and in the years of famine Egypt will not go hungry. Pharaoh, you must appoint a wise man to take charge of all this.'

Pharaoh descended from his throne and embraced Joseph. 'Of course! Of course! I understand those dreams now. You have saved our country from ruin! Can any man be greater than this? You must be the one to carry this out.'

He was so grateful to Joseph that he made him governor of Egypt and gave him his own gold chain studded with amber, fine clothing to wear, a golden carriage to ride in. The people of Egypt lined the streets to see the famous magician. 'Abrek! Abrek!' they were told. 'Bend your knee to the great master.' No one except Pharaoh himself was more important or more powerful, and nothing could happen anywhere in the country without Joseph's permission.

During the seven years of plenty Joseph worked very hard. He ordered the building of huge granaries in every city. When the corn in the fields was as high as a man and as golden as the sun he set the reapers to bring in the harvest. It was like sand from the sea shore, there was so much of it, yet he appointed tellers to count it and store and stack it. He knew exactly how much there was, and where it was kept. Nothing was wasted, and the people were allowed just as much as they needed to live on and no more. Because he was so well-loved and respected they did exactly as he told them.

And then the famine came. Day after day the sun scorched down, and no rain came. The Nile shrank in its bed; the earth was parched, the corn withered on cracked stalks. Winter brought shrill winds that blasted the fields so nothing could be sewn or harvested. Egypt fainted with hunger. Then Joseph allowed the stored grain to be rationed out; only as much as people needed to stay alive. It had to last for seven years; he knew that because God had told him.

The famine was not only in Egypt. It was world-wide. Only Egypt had stores of grain. Traders from other famished countries travelled there offering money, spices, nuts, perfumes, silver; anything in exchange for grain to make their bread. And among them were ten brothers from Canaan.

When they were ushered in to see Joseph to plead their case, he recognized them at once. The memory of their cruelty washed through him like nausea. He sat on his throne watching them as they kissed the ground at his feet. They had no idea he was their brother. He was a man now, not a Hebrew shepherd boy called Joseph but a great Egyptian ruler called Zaphenath-Paneah. He spoke to them through an interpreter, so they wouldn't realize that he understood their language. And he smiled to himself. He could play games with them now. He could punish them for the way they had treated him in Canaan. He could do anything he wanted with them.

'These men are spies,' he said to the guards. 'Put them in prison.'

The ten brothers begged for mercy, but he refused to listen to them, and the guards dragged them away and threw them into the dark cells. After three days they were brought before Joseph again.

'What do you have to say for yourselves?' he asked, still enjoying his game.

'We're not spies. We are ten brothers,' Reuben pleaded again.

'We have good silver to pay for grain. We have heard that Egypt has huge supplies. Our families are starving.'

Joseph closed his eyes. He was overwhelmed with nostalgia for that old forgotten way of life, shepherding in the hills, sleeping in goatskin tents, eating under the stars. 'Who is your father?' he asked.

'Our father is called Jacob. He's too old to travel here himself.'

So his father was still alive. It was his first news from home for over ten years. Now he was hungry for more. 'Who else is there?'

'One young brother, Benjamin.'

Joseph felt his throat tightening. How he would love to see Benjamin again.

'Why isn't he with you?' he asked.

'Our father would not let him travel with us,' Simeon told him. 'He's too well-loved, too precious. We had another younger brother, you see, called Joseph, but he's dead.'

'Dead!' repeated Joseph. 'Well, I don't know whether to believe your story or not. I'll send you back with food, as you're starving, but one of you will stay here as a hostage.' He pointed at Simeon. 'You stay here. When your brothers bring me Benjamin, I'll believe you're not spies and release you.'

'Father will never let Benjamin come here,' Simeon said, struggling as the guards tied him up and led him away. 'I'll rot in prison and never see any of you again.'

'This is our punishment, for what we did to Joseph all those years ago,' Judah said to his brothers. He had no idea that the man on the throne spoke perfect Hebrew and could understand everything he said. Joseph was full of pity for himself and for them, but he hardened his heart.

'Fetch Benjamin,' he ordered, and walked away from them.

When the nine brothers arrived back in Canaan they unloaded the bags of corn from their donkeys and discovered that the money that they had given in exchange was still there, hidden in the corn. They looked at each other, troubled by this, weak with fear for what it might mean. They went to their father and told him of the strange ways of Zaphenath-Paneah. And then they broke the terrible news that he had put Simeon in prison and ordered them to take Benjamin to Egypt.

Simeon was right. Jacob was shocked and bitter at the loss of his son, but he refused to let them take Benjamin to Egypt.

'I have lost Joseph, I have lost Simeon, and now you're asking me to send Benjamin away. I won't do it. I can't. It would break my heart to let him go.'

But soon the corn they had brought from Egypt was used up and they were all starving again. Judah begged Jacob to let them go back to Egypt to buy more food, and to let Benjamin go with them.

'If we don't go to Egypt, we'll all die,' he said. 'But Benjamin will have to come with us.'

Jacob broke down and cried in his son's arms. 'I'm an old man. If Benjamin doesn't come home I'll die of grief.'

'We'll bring him home,' Reuben promised. 'If we don't, you may take my own two sons and slay them. You have my word, father.'

So they travelled back to Egypt with double the amount of money, and presents of pistachio nuts and almonds and honey, things that couldn't be found in Egypt, hoping to please the governor. Joseph was watching out for them and when he was told of their arrival from Canaan he sent his steward to bring them to his house. The brothers were afraid, thinking that they were going to be punished because of the money that had been found in their sacks.

'We didn't steal it, but we have brought more money with us to replace it and to buy food.'

But the steward refused to take the money and told them not to worry, and so they took their presents to Joseph's house and waited for him to come home at noon.

The first thing Joseph asked them when he came home was, 'Is your father well?' His interpreter repeated the words in Hebrew.

'Yes, but very sad to let Benjamin go,' Judah replied.

'Where is he?' Joseph asked.

'This is Benjamin.' Reuben pointed to a boy on a donkey. Benjamin wasn't a little child any longer, but a fine young man. Joseph was so moved that he went back to his room and threw himself on his bed and wept; it was almost more than he could bear. Nothing that had happened to him in Egypt was more wonderful than seeing his younger brother again. Gradually his storm of emotion calmed, and he lay on his bed, thinking what to do next. He had been given the power to save Egypt, and now he had the power to save the father and brother who really loved him.

First, he released Simeon from prison, as he had promised. He ordered the brothers' horses and donkey to be loaded up with sacks of corn with each man's money in the top of his sack. Then, the night before they left for home, he invited all the brothers to dine with him. They marvelled at the pillared courtyards filled with fruit trees and gleaming ponds, and the luxury of the banqueting hall where the feast was held.

'You've shown us great hospitality,' Reuben said. 'If our old father was well enough he would want to come here to thank you himself.'

'I wish he was here with you,' Joseph said. 'With all my heart I wish that.' He lifted up his silver wine goblet and passed it to Benjamin, smiling at the way the boy turned it round in his hands to admire the pearls and jewels on it before he drank.

The next day Joseph secretly instructed one of the servants to hide the precious goblet in Benjamin's sack. The brothers rode away, thankful that everything had gone well and that they would soon be home again with their news of the extraordinary hospitality of Zaphenath-Paneah. But they had hardly lost sight of the beautiful city when they heard the sound of horses' hooves pounding across the sand. Egyptian guards were riding after them, shouting at them to stop, and to empty out their sacks of corn.

'Why have you been so wicked when so much good has been done to you?' the chief guard demanded. 'Someone has stolen the governor's goblet. Whoever it is will be made to be his servant.'

The brothers willingly allowed their sacks to be emptied, promising that there had been some mistake, that none of them would dream of stealing anything. But to their horror the goblet was found in Benjamin's sack. They couldn't believe it.

'I didn't steal it, I wouldn't, I couldn't!' Benjamin cried, but the guards bundled him up onto one of their horses and galloped back to the city with him. He was bewildered and frightened and kept twisting round on the horse, shouting to his brothers to come and rescue him before Zaphenath-Paneah had him beheaded.

His brothers were wretched with grief. 'How can we go home without Benjamin?' Judah asked. 'This will kill our father. He'll die of sorrow.'

They followed the guards back to the city and one after another they begged Joseph to be merciful.

'Zaphenath-Paneah, please listen to us. Our brother is innocent.'

'Let me take Benjamin's place. I'll be your slave.'

'Our old father will die of sorrow if Benjamin stays with you.'

'He's the child of his old age, the only remaining son from his second wife.'

'He's already lost Joseph. He loved them both, and now he must lose them both.'

'And it will break his heart.'

Joseph felt as if his own heart was breaking. He sent all the servants and guards away so that he was alone with his eleven brothers, and then he spoke to them in Hebrew and told them the truth.

'I am the brother with the coat of the colour of pomegranates, that our father gave to me. I am the brother who was cast into a pit to die. I am the brother who was sold into slavery in Egypt.'

They stared at him in disbelief. Could this great and powerful man really be Joseph? But if it wasn't, how could he know these things?

'Joseph!' Benjamin said.

They all went down on their knees to Joseph, and he took each of them by the hand and made them stand again, and spoke to each of them by name: 'Reuben, Simeon, Levi, Judah, Isaachar, Zebulun, Dan, Naphtali, Gad, Asher, Benjamin, don't be afraid, don't be ashamed. Such good has come of it. It was God's will that I should come here to help you in the time of famine. Tell my father this. There's nothing more I want now than to have my whole family here with me, to make your home in Egypt and to live together again. I want to see my father again before he dies.'

Joseph sent horses and chariots and wagons to Canaan to bring his brothers' wives and children and all the old people to Egypt. He waited alone in his room, watching out for the clouds of sand-dust on the horizon, and when he saw them he ran out to meet the chariots. Jacob climbed down, old and weak and trembling, and stared for a long time at Joseph.

'Yes,' he said at last. 'You are Joseph. You are my son.'

They put their arms round each other and wept for the lost years, and laughed for the great joy of being together again, father and son.

Moses, the Child of the River

Old Jacob was known as Israel now. He and all his children and all their families were given land in a part of Egypt called Goshen to set up their tents. This is how they had always lived and this was how they wanted to live now, as shepherds and farmers. But here the land was rich and fertile, irrigated by canals from the Red Sea. And here in Goshen they grew and multiplied, as God had promised Abraham, for generation after generation.

Many years passed, and in all that time the Israelites lived in peace. But then Pharaoh Rameses the second came to the throne. He was more ambitious than any other ruler had been, and he made Egypt into a powerful civilization. Great cities were built, with huge statues of himself erected at the gates, and avenues of stone sphinxes, which had the bodies of lions and the faces of men, to represent strength and wisdom. All this was to show the rest of the world that the Egyptians were superior to any other nation.

But there was a group of people in Egypt who were not Egyptian, who had nothing to do with Egyptian life. They had their own language and their own culture, and they worshipped their own god. These were the Israelites of Goshen, and there were huge numbers of them. Pharaoh Rameses called them the Hebrews, and he was frightened that there would soon be more Hebrews than Egyptians in his country. He knew that he had to do something about it before it was too late.

'The Hebrews must go,' he told the officers of his army. 'Send them out of Egypt. They don't belong here.'

'Is that a good idea?' his advisers asked. 'There are many thousands of them. They might join forces with one of our enemies and invade us.'

'Then make them work for us!' Rameses shouted. 'Turn them into slaves, and make them work till they're on their knees. Beat them and starve them, but make them work.'

His soldiers marched into Goshen and hauled the Israelite men away from their families, and led them away in work gangs to dig canals and dams, to toil in brickyards and building sites, building the temples and houses that showed the world what a glorious country Egypt was. Every brick they made was stamped with the symbol of Rameses, every temple and statue covered with hieroglyphs in a language that the Israelite builders did not even know.

Still the Israelites multiplied, and at last Rameses said, 'Enough! I have had enough of these Hebrew people. They swarm through the streets like desert rats. We must stop them breeding. We must drown every Hebrew boy child that is born from now on.'

The Egyptian women and midwives were shocked that their pharaoh could think of such a cruel thing, and when they were ordered to drown the boy babies from the slaves' shacks they pretended not to understand. But they were punished if they did not follow the word of Pharaoh. Many, many of the boy babies that were born in that time were thrown in the Nile.

But one of the babies survived, and became the leader of his people. This is his story.

His mother already had a little boy called Aaron and a little girl called Miriam. When her new baby son was born she knew that his life was in danger; she was terrified that he might be found by Egyptian soldiers and killed. She managed to hide him for three months, stifling his cries with kisses, telling Aaron and Miriam to make as much noise as they could. But the time came when he was too big to hide, and she knew that at any moment the soldiers would come for him.

'Anything would be better than watching Pharaoh's soldiers take him,' his mother said. 'We must let our baby go, Miriam.'

Together they plaited the bark of the papyrus tree and made a tiny ark for him. They slimed it with tar to make it watertight. Then they set the little ark among the rustling reeds and bulrushes that grew out of the river Nile.

'May you sink or may you swim, as God wills it,' the mother whispered to her baby. 'But I will never see you again, for I can't bear to watch them drown you.'

Miriam stayed behind long after her mother had run home in distress. She hid herself on the river bank in a clump of bulrushes and watched the little ark bobbing on the water. She knew there was nothing she could do to help the baby, but she couldn't bring herself to leave him there all on his own.

If she hadn't stayed, she would never have known the wonderful thing that happened to her little brother.

Later that day, Pharaoh's daughter came down to the Nile to bathe. She was surrounded by her maids, who were carrying fans of ostrich feathers to cool her in the baking heat. She heard something crying and thought it was a river bird, and then she heard it again, coming from a bed of bulrushes.

'It sounds just like a baby,' she told her maids. 'Go and see.'

When they brought the ark to her she lifted the lid and saw that it was true, that a frightened baby was wrapped inside, hungry and crying

for his mother. She lifted him out and cradled him in her arms, and she ached with pity for him.

'It's a Hebrew baby,' she said. 'Poor little child. Don't tell anyone about this, will you? I must take him home and find someone to look after him. We can't leave him here to die.'

Miriam couldn't bear to keep quiet any longer. She crept out of her hiding place and ran to the princess. 'Princess, I know a Hebrew woman who could feed him and look after him for you,' she said. Her heart was thudding like a drum with fear and excitement.

The princess looked down at the little girl and smiled. Maybe she understood who that Hebrew woman might be, maybe she didn't, but she agreed to let Miriam fetch her mother and bring her to her palace.

'I want you to look after my baby,' the princess said. 'I am going to call him Moses, child of the river. He will be a prince in my household, but you must care for him as if he were your own son.'

So that is how Moses the Israelite, child of a Hebrew slave, became a royal prince in the court of the pharaoh of Egypt. And later he became one of the most powerful men of all time.

Moses and the Pharaoh

So Moses was brought up as an Egyptian in the court of Pharaoh's daughter. He could have anything he wanted, and he saw his brother Aaron and sister Miriam from time to time, when his mother was allowed to bring them to the gardens to speak to him. He was quite shy, and his speech was slow, but he learnt the things that other Egyptian boys learn, all the science and literature of a great nation, and the princess was very proud of him. But his nurse, his real mother, never let him forget that he was really a Hebrew, son of the people of Abraham and Isaac and Jacob. He prayed to his own God, and never worshipped at the Egyptian temples.

It must have been strange for him, brought up as a pampered child of the court, to see how cruelly his own people were treated. He had only to ride through the streets in his chariot to see the Hebrew labourers heaving logs and stones on ropes, sweating in brickyards in the torrid heat of the day while their taskmasters forced them on to work harder and faster. Then, one day, his temper got the better of him. He saw a Hebrew slave being whipped because he was too weak to work. Moses' anger rose up in him like a wild beast. He leapt down from his chariot and killed the Egyptian.

When he realized what he had done he panicked. He had never done anything like this before; he was a favoured son of Pharaoh's court, and now he had killed a man. He cried with shame because of what his anger had caused him to do, and yet he was afraid of what might happen to him now. Desperately he covered the body with sand, but even before he had returned to the palace a man called out to him that he was a murderer. He daren't go home again now. He ran away from Egypt into another country, far from the rich courts of his childhood, and lived the simple life of a shepherd. He married a farmer's daughter, and would have lived quite happily for the rest of his life.

But God had great plans for him, and great talents to give him. The old pharaoh of Egypt had died, but his successor was even more cruel than he had been. God heard the anguish of the Hebrew slaves in Egypt, and he thought of a way to save them. But first he had to make Moses more powerful than any magician in Pharaoh's court.

Moses was watching his flock of goats in a quiet valley under the towering rocks of Mount Sinai when suddenly he saw a bush catch fire. Flames tore through the branches, and the bush blazed with light, but, amazingly, it didn't burn. It stayed upright, strong and supple; every leaf glowed with separate tongues of flame, but they didn't curl up or blacken with scorch. The heat of the fire was so intense that Moses cowered away from it; flames poured from the tree, yet the tree was lush and strong. Then he heard the voice of God, coming from the heart of the fire, and he knew that he was in a holy place, and that this wonder was for him alone.

Moses, Moses, know who I am.

I am the God of Abraham,

of Isaac and of Jacob.

I have heard their children crying in Egypt.

I know their sorrow.

I made a promise,

and it is time to keep my word.

They will go to the Promised Land.

And you will lead them there.

Moses knelt down in the sand.

'Me?' he protested. 'But I'm just a goat-herd! Pharaoh won't listen to me! He'll never let them go.'

I will use all my wonders.

I will pour curses on Pharaoh, on his people and his land.

And when he can take no more, then he will let my people go.

Lead them, Moses.

Lead them out of slavery

to the land of milk and honey.

Moses protested again. He was weak with fear and strong with wonder, both at the same time. 'Why should the Hebrew slaves follow me? They know I was brought up as an Egyptian. They will think I am just like Pharaoh. They will never believe that you have told me to do these things.'

What do you hold in your hand, Moses?

'This?' Moses laughed, puzzled. 'This is my shepherd's staff, that's all.'

Throw it to the ground.

Moses did as God said, and the staff turned into a snake, hissing and writhing in the sand.

Now pick it up, Moses.

'Pick up a snake? But it might kill me!'

Moses cautiously stretched out his hand, and the snake turned back into a shepherd's staff.

'That is true power,' he breathed.

The power is in your own hand.

Look at it, Moses.

Moses looked down and saw the hand of a leper, scaled like a fish with silvery flakes, and as pale as death. And as he looked, it became his own hand again, firm and strong.

Everything I say to you

will give you greater power

than any magician in Pharaoh's court.

Use my power, call it magic, call it miracle,

but lead my people out of Egypt, Moses.

But still Moses shook his head in disbelief. 'I won't be able to persuade them to come with me. I'm tongue-tied, I don't have the words to make them listen.'

Your brother will speak for you.

You will give him the words I give to you.

You will give him the wonders I give to you.

Speak to Pharaoh; show him my power,

and I will harden his heart till his sorrow

is greater than the sorrow of all my children.

Then lead my people out of Egypt.

They shall receive a glorious kingdom.

Lead them, Moses.

The fire faded, and in its place stood the live bush, gleaming green and strong. The sheep grazed quietly round it as though nothing had happened. Moses called them together and went from that holy place, and his heart was full of mystery and power. He told his wife and children that he must leave them for a while because he had God's work to do, and then he set off across the miles and miles of sandhills that would take him back to Egypt. On his way he saw his brother Aaron, who was a high priest by now, and he ran to him and told him what had happened.

'Aaron, Aaron, I've seen God!' he shouted, stammering because he was so full of the wonderful story he had to tell. 'He's given me magic powers, and I must share them with you.'

Aaron laughed. 'I wish I could believe you, Moses.'

'Listen! I made my wooden stick writhe and wriggle in the sand. It really happened—it was a snake! Then I saw my flesh wither and die and come to life again. Honestly, I've seen God.'

When Aaron saw how serious his brother was, he believed that Moses must be telling the truth, though he didn't understand it. He put his arms round him, and in that embrace God let Aaron share the power he had given to Moses.

'Tell me what you have to do, and I'll help you,' he promised.

'We must go to Pharaoh now and ask him to free the Hebrew slaves,' Moses said. 'But you have to do the talking, Aaron. You know how tongue-tied I get.'

They crossed the desert together and went straight to Pharaoh, and asked to speak to him. They were eventually ushered into the great court that Moses had known as a child. But this Pharaoh did not know him, and Moses had no wish to be treated as an Egyptian. They bowed to their ruler, and then Aaron looked at Moses and read in his eyes what he wanted to say.

'We speak as Hebrews, not as Egyptians,' Aaron said. 'Pharaoh, we ask you to let our people go.'

'God sent us,' Moses stammered.

'God sent you!' Pharaoh repeated scornfully. 'Your god means nothing to me. Go away!'

He ordered the taskmasters to be stricter than ever. The slaves in the brickyards were forced to find their own straw for brickmaking, and yet make just as many as they had before. They had to work twice as hard, and when they sank to their knees with weakness they were whipped. 'Show them no mercy!' he shouted. 'These people are my slaves. How dare they ask for freedom!'

Aaron and Moses watched helplessly, but they knew they couldn't give up. They ran through the narrow alleys where the Hebrew people lived, and called the slaves out of their hovels.

'We will leave Egypt one day soon,' Aaron told them. 'Trust Moses. One day he will take us to the Promised Land, the land of milk and honey.'

The slaves looked wonderingly at Moses. Could he really do this for them, they asked each other, and shook their heads. But all the same, Aaron's promise was like a spoken dream, and it put a flicker of hope into their hearts.

Next day Moses and Aaron went back to Pharaoh.

'How dare you come here again?' he demanded.

'We have the power to make you listen to us,' Aaron said. He and Moses threw their staffs on the mosaic floor in front of Pharaoh. The staffs turned to snakes, coiling and slithering on the ground. But Pharaoh sent for his wizards and conjurors, and they did the same thing. Their staffs writhed on the ground around the feet of Moses. Pharaoh's magicians laughed.

'This is easy magic, Pharaoh,' they said.

But Aaron's snake reared its head and ate up all their snakes. Pharaoh saw then that Aaron and Moses were more powerful than his own magicians.

'Now will you let our people go?' Aaron demanded.

Pharaoh was afraid of them both, but he hardened his heart against them.

'No, I will not let your people go,' he said.

'Then I will show you the power that God has given me.' Moses closed his eyes and knew what he must do. He stretched out his hand towards the mighty Nile, and all the waters of Egypt turned into blood; the rivers, the streams, the lakes, the ponds that the animals drank from, the pools in the gardens, the little drops inside the pockets of stones and logs, the dew that dangled from grasses—all turned thick and crimson. The fishes drowned in blood, and lay stinking on the banks.

But Pharaoh called his wizards, and they showed that they could do the same thing by turning the water in the drinking cups to blood.

'Magic for magic,' he snarled. 'No, I will not let your people go.'

Moses turned to his brother, and Aaron stretched out his hand towards the Nile, and frogs came out of the water, and more frogs, and more, thousands after thousands, armies of frogs, and they hopped down the streets and into the houses, into the people's beds, into the vats of flour. But the wizards of Pharaoh did the same thing, till there were more frogs than people. The Egyptians begged the wizards to stop, and Moses lifted his hand and brought death on all the frogs.

But still Pharaoh hardened his heart against him. 'No,' he said, 'I will not let your people go.'

Aaron and Moses took a handful of dust and threw it into the air, and as it fell it turned into hundreds and thousands of lice; lice everywhere, crawling and clinging on to men and beasts, fastening like buttons on their flesh, sucking their blood. Pharaoh turned to his wizards, but they shook their heads.

'This is more powerful than any magic we can do,' they said.

'Let my people go,' said Moses.

And still Pharaoh hardened his heart, and said, 'No.'

And so the brothers conjured up a swarm of flies that came soundlessly into the ears and the hair and the eyes of every Egyptian, and stabbed them with tiny needles of poison, and sucked their blood. Pharaoh was covered in them—the more he brushed away, the more swarmed round him again. They were in his clothes and in his bed, in the kitchens; everywhere.

'Yes, yes,' Pharaoh said, flapping his hands uselessly round his face. 'Do anything, go, but rid us of these flies.'

Moses spoke to the flies, and they all slumbered into death. But as soon as the whining had stopped, as soon as the itching had stopped, Pharaoh hardened his heart against Moses. He hated the Hebrews more than ever, he wanted to punish them, not give them freedom.

'No,' he said. 'I've changed my mind. I will not let your people go.'

The farmers ran out of their fields and pastures crying to him that all their sheep and cattle were covered in boils. The boils burst and maggots crawled into them, and the beasts swayed down onto their knees and died.

'Now,' said Moses. 'Let us go.'

But Pharaoh hated Moses even more for bringing the plagues down on him. No, his heart was hardened against him, he would not let him go, do what he would, he would never let the Hebrew slaves go.

Aaron took a handful of ashes and threw them into the air, and they drifted down on the Egyptians and covered them all with painful boils that throbbed and oozed and burst and throbbed again. All Pharaoh's subjects begged him to change his mind and do as the two brothers said. Even his wizards came to him on their knees and pleaded with him.

'There is no magic stronger than this,' they said. 'Let the slaves go.'

But Pharaoh's heart was as hard as stone. No, he would not let them go.

The next day fire ran along the ground like a red tongue of hunger, devouring everything in its path, and then the sky froze and dropped stones of ice onto Egypt. Every man who was not hiding was killed, every beast, every tree and plant was flattened, every house battered like paper. All night and all day the sound of hail thudding on the earth was like the beating of remorseless drums.

Pharaoh looked round at the devastation of his country and called Moses to him. He had to shout to make himself heard over the noise of the thunder and the hail. 'I'm sorry for my sins. I'm sorry for my cruelty to your people. Yes, I will let them go.'

But as soon as Moses caused the hailstorm to die away, Pharaoh breathed in the blessed silence and broke his word. His heart was as hard as the hail had been.

'No,' he said. 'Your people cannot go. Never. They belong to me.'

So an east wind howled for a day and a night and a day and a night, and when it had gone, a cloud of locusts came like shadows of death across the sky. They swarmed across the earth of Egypt and ate up every green plant that was still growing on it.

'Let the slaves go,' Pharaoh's people begged him. 'Egypt is dead.'

Pharaoh turned to Moses and said, 'You can go.'

A soft west wind breathed into the clouds of locusts and blew them away from Egypt into the Red Sea. And as soon as they had gone, Pharaoh called Moses to him and laughed in his face.

'You are still mine,' he said. 'Mine for ever.'

Moses was weary. He turned to his brother, and Aaron summoned up his greatest power yet. He stretched out his hand and the sun turned black. Darkness covered the land. No Egyptian could see his own hand, or his wife or his child; they groped in the thick darkness and knew nothing but fear. And with the darkness came a silence that could be felt, like a blanket of heavy wool. But the Hebrews walked in light and sunshine.

For three days the darkness lasted, and when it was lifted Pharaoh said, 'You can go, all of you can go, but not your cattle. We need them, because our own are dead. But go; get out of my sight. If I see you again, you will die.'

But God was not ready to forgive Pharaoh yet. It was a time for the worst punishment that could be imagined, worse than any of the plagues that had been inflicted on the people and the land of the Egyptians. God had no mercy against them, but he wanted to spare the Israelites, so he spoke into Moses' heart.

Tell every Israelite family to kill a lamb
and put a mark upon their door with blood,
so I will know my chosen people.
So I will spare them, my chosen people.
For in the night I will pass over their houses.
In the night I will enter all other houses
and kill every first-born child in Egypt.

That night, the night of the Passover, the Israelites feasted. Every household slaughtered their best lamb and roasted it over the fire with herbs. They ate it with unleavened bread, and then they smeared their doors with blood from the lamb, so the angel of death would pass over them and not breathe on their children. And they waited for what they knew was going to happen.

The night was as black as the bed of the deepest ocean. God swept down on Egypt with a strike of searing light, and at that moment a great cry of grief was heard over the whole of Egypt. Every first child in every house died, except the children of the slaves. No one could save them and no one could hide them, and no one could silence the sorrow of Egypt.

The lamentations of the Egyptians seared the morning with grief. At last Pharaoh understood that the vengeance of God was greater than the magic of any wizard or the power of any man on earth. His spirit was broken.

'Go,' he said. 'Truly, you can go out of Egypt. Take the old and the young, the women and children, the cattle and the sheep and the goats. Take your people and go.'

Parting the Waves

Moses opened up the tomb of Joseph and brought out his bones so that the people of Israel would not be leaving their ancestor behind. Then he called together all the slaves, all six hundred thousand of them.

'Our time has come,' he said.

They collected up their belongings, their warm rugs and their wooden cooking utensils, and gathered outside Goshen as Moses had asked them to. When the Egyptians saw them coming together they pressed jewellery, silver, gold into their hands, released their cattle and sheep from the fields, gave them mules and camels and horses to ride on, so glad were they to see them go. Moses led his people past the soldiers, past the fortresses and the lookout towers, and nobody made any attempt to stop him. They were truly free.

A spiralling cloud twisted and swirled ahead of them. It was a terrifying and wonderful thing to see—a sand angel that was made of golden light. At night the whirlwind burned like a torch to guide them. It led the tribe of Israelites down to the Red Sea, weaving a path across the desert that made them wander backwards and forwards as if they had mistaken their way. When Pharaoh heard about this he thought that the Israelites were lost in the wilderness, and that even now he could get his revenge on them for the plagues that had ravaged Egypt and killed his own first child.

He followed them with six hundred chariots of soldiers. From far away in the shimmer of the sand he could see their makeshift tents set up on the shores of the Red Sea.

'We'll chase them into the sea,' he laughed. 'And there they will die.

Every man and woman, every child and beast. The sea will cover them, and the shame of Pharaoh will be forgotten for ever.'

The Israelites gazed across the reedy waters in despair and disbelief. There was no way across, yet behind them they could hear the pounding of hundreds of horses in the desert. The sky was thick with the clouds of sand, and through the clouds came the gleam of armour. The air rang with the shouts of the Egyptian soldiers.

'Have you brought us here to die?' the frightened Israelites asked Moses.

'Roll up your tents, and gather together the beasts,' he told them. 'We must cross the water.'

But the sea stretched ahead of them, and they had no way of crossing it. Nearer and nearer the horses and chariots pounded; louder and fiercer rang the voices of the Egyptians.

'Must we run into the sea and drown?'

'Trust me. I will lead you,' Moses promised, repeating the words that God spoke to him. He stretched out his hand towards the sea. It was still and calm, a perfect mirror of the sky. And yet, as the Israelites watched, a dark line ran from the far distant shore towards them, creasing the surface of the water, and as it ran it seemed to rip the sea into two halves. Waves plunged away from either side of the line and then, suddenly, the sea was divided and a dry path lay where the water had been. Towering waves tossed and reared on either side like wild horses.

As quickly as they could the Israelites rolled up their tents and heaped their belongings onto the horses and mules. They herded up their animals and drove them onto the path behind Moses. And still the thundering hooves approached. They ran along the dry path between the quivering walls of water, glancing fearfully behind them. The far shore stretched out like open arms.

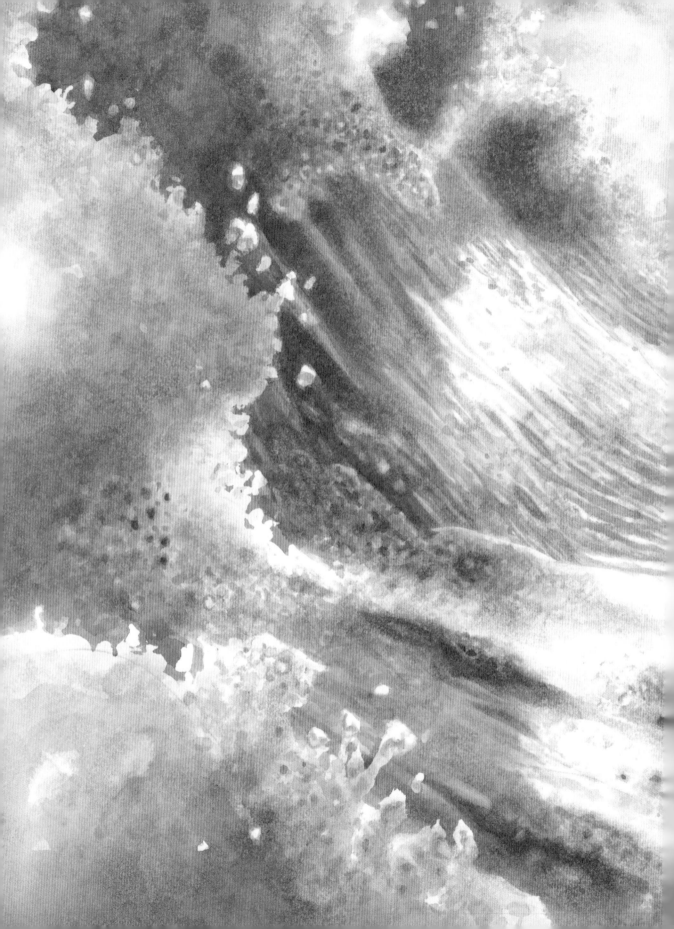

As they came nearer, the Egyptian army could see the Israelites walking into the sea and thought that they must have found a causeway of some sort to walk along. Pharaoh urged his soldiers on.

'We have them now!' he shouted. 'Draw your swords!'

They whipped their horses on, and suddenly they were engulfed in a whirlwind of dense black cloud. They plunged on into God's darkness, with the wild sea towering on either side of them.

'Forward, forward!' Pharaoh cried.

They were nearly halfway across when the very last of the Israelites reached the safety of the far shore. Moses turned towards the sea and lifted his hand. And the sea fell. Like the walls of a plundered city, the waves crashed down. The Egyptian soldiers screamed in panic. The wheels of their chariots sank into the mud; they could move neither forward nor backwards. The frightened soldiers jumped from the chariots with their swords in their hands, and every one of them twisted and turned and sank deep under the sea, tangled in reeds and the reins of their horses. And they lay still at last; horses and soldiers still in the sleep of the drowned.

On the far shore, the Israelites went on their knees and thanked God. Miriam, the sister of Moses, sang and danced and shook the bells of her tambourine.

'God is a God of war.

He has drowned the horses

He has drowned the riders

He has drowned the soldiers of Pharaoh of Egypt

They have sunk like stones to the bed of the sea.'

That was her song and all the children of Israel sang it with her, rejoicing in the terrible marvel that had happened. They believed at last that they were God's chosen people.

When they reached the land of Midian, Moses ran ahead of them to find the farm where he had lived with Jethro's family. After the years of separation and anguish, he and his wife were together again. He folded his children in his arms. They could only just remember him, the shepherd father who had left them behind so he could do God's work.

'My work isn't finished yet,' he told them. He looked round at the soft hills and fields that he had loved so much when he was first married. How he would love to have that simple life again. 'We can't stay here. We have to travel on to the land God has prepared for us. We can build our homes there, and live in peace.'

And so he led them on, and for many weeks the Israelites wandered, from dry river bed to parched mountainside, and found no place to make their home. The people were restless and angry with Moses. The desert was a harsh place to live in; the sand lashed them like whips, the sun blistered their skin every day and at night the stars brought bitter cold. There was no water fit to drink, they were wretched with hunger. They were afraid of bandits and poisonous snakes.

'Even living as slaves in Egypt was better than this,' they complained. 'What's going to happen to us now?'

Moses found little white seeds of manna that God had sent for them.

'Here's bread from heaven,' he told them. 'As sweet as honey to sip.' He found flocks of tiny quails for them to eat. With God's help he turned poisoned wells into pure drinking water, and still they complained bitterly.

'We never wanted to live in the desert. This is no home for us. When will you take us to the Promised Land?' they demanded. 'We don't believe in it any more. We don't believe in you.'

And when he reminded them that God was among them, they refused to believe that, either.

Wearily, they set up their tents again in the Sinai Mountains. It was here, long ago in the valley below Mount Sinai, that Moses had seen the burning bush, when the voice of God had told him to bring his people out of Egypt. The place was desolate now. The mountain brooded over them. Eagles screamed from the crags, and the cold wind whined round the valley. Moses gazed round in despair. How could he prove that what he said was true?

As the sun went down, Mount Sinai blazed with crimson light. Suddenly the summit went black. Thunder rolled, lightning tore the sky into shreds, the mountain belched fire and smoke. Moses stood up and heard the voice of God inside his head.

I am the lord your God.

These are my commandments to you . . .

Moses climbed up through the storm cloud to the summit of the mountain, and there he found two stones that were engraved with the laws of God, telling people how they must live with each other and with God himself. These were the Ten Commandments of God:

I am the lord your God. You shall not worship any other god but me.
You shall not worship any statue or picture.
You shall speak my name with great reverence.
You shall keep the seventh day holy, for when I made the world, I rested on that day.
You shall honour your father and your mother.
You shall not commit murder.
You shall not be unfaithful to your husband or wife.

You shall not steal.
You shall not lie about any person.
You shall not envy anybody's possessions.

For forty days and forty nights Moses fasted on the summit of Mount Horeb. Down in the valley below the Israelites were restless and angry. They thought he had deserted them, and they had no idea what to do next. They turned to Aaron, but while Moses was up among the mountains of Sinai his brother Aaron committed a great wrong. He remembered the power he had had from God when he had helped his brother to defeat the magicians of Pharaoh's court, and he wanted it back again. Everyone had looked up at him and admired him and loved him, but now that power was gone; his brother had gone, and it seemed as if his God had gone.

'We'll make a new god,' he promised. 'We'll make it ourselves and worship it.'

The idea was exciting; it gave the weary people something to think about, something to do. They gathered together all the bits and pieces of gold that they were wearing, ear-rings and bracelets that the Egyptians had given them, and they melted them down and carved a bull out of it. Then they built an altar and lit fires round the bull, and daubed their faces with ashes and blood and danced round and round it until they were dizzy. They were in a trance, swaying together, chanting and moaning round the statue, when Moses came down at last from Mount Sinai.

It was night time. He was carrying the two slabs containing the written word of God in his arms, and his face glowed with the joy of what he had to give his people. If they had been watching out for him they would have seen him coming towards them like a bright light in the darkness. But no one was watching.

As he approached the camp he could not believe what he could hear and see, what had happened to the Israelites in his absence. They were dancing round a false god; they were naked and smeared with the blood of sacrificed animals. They were breaking the very first of God's commandments. He threw down the tablets of stone, and they smashed into little pieces. He roared with sorrow; he went on his knees and wept.

Then he broke the golden bull and stamped out the fires, and the people watched him in silent shame.

'Even my brother has failed me,' Moses said bitterly. 'I shared my power with him, and he has failed me. Will no man stand by me now?'

Some of the men stepped forward and stood next to him.

'I must ask you to prove your loyalty to me and to God,' he said to them. 'I must ask each of you to kill anyone who is not on our side, even if he is your own brother.'

There was a gasp of horror, but he went on, 'You must do this to prove your loyalty to me. You must do it to show that you understand how greatly you have sinned. You must do it to show God you are sorry.'

So the men did what he wanted, and nobody stopped them, and many were killed that night. But Aaron was spared, and became high priest.

God spoke to Moses again and told him to cut two more tablets of stone, so the commandments could be written as before. He told him to come on his own at dawn to the summit of Mount Sinai, and there in the first green light of day, God appeared.

Moses, I am the Lord.

I am merciful,

I am slow to anger

and full of love.

I forgive sin.

Even though I make men pay

for the sins of their fathers

their grandfathers

their great-grandfathers

in the end, I forgive.

I will help you defeat your enemies

and will prepare a way to the land I have promised

for you are my chosen people—

and you must obey my commandments.

This is the agreement I will make—

this is my covenant—

with you, Moses, and with the people of Israel.

Now everyone came together again under Moses' leadership. God asked them to build an Ark of the Covenant to keep safe the stones. It took many years to make. The Ark was made of acacia wood and covered with gold, and when it was finished it was placed inside a gorgeous tabernacle, a tent made by a man called Bezalel. This tabernacle was gold inside and outside, and hung with onyx stones, topaz, emeralds, sapphires, diamonds, agate, amethyst, beryl, jasper, so it glimmered with colours like a garden of jewels. It was decorated with golden bells and grapes and pomegranates, and when it was finished God breathed himself into it. It was filled with him like the smoke of incense.

The tabernacle was the size of a huge temple. It would take many hundreds of men to lift it, but the Israelites vowed to carry it with them wherever they went, because God was inside it.

And when the tabernacle was ready, they lifted it up and set off again on their search for the Promised Land.

A Land of Milk and Honey

At last the Israelites drew within sight of the Promised Land, but still God would not let them enter.

He told Moses to choose twelve men from the twelve tribes of the Israelites, and send them as spies into Canaan, so Moses would know what the country was like. The twelve tribes were all descended from the twelve sons of Jacob: Reuben, Simeon, Judah, Isaachar, Ephraim, Zebulun, Dan, Asher, Napthali, Gad, Joseph, and Benjamin. From these twelve tribes Moses elected Shammua, Shaphar, Igal, Palti, Gaddiel, Gaddi, Ammeil, Sethur, Nahbi, Geuel, Caleb, and Joshua.

'Climb the hills of Canaan and enter the land below,' he told them. 'Find out everything you can about it. See what the soil is like; whether it is fertile or poor. See what the people are like, are they strong or weak, many or few? See what the towns are like, and whether we will take them easily or by force. Find out all these things and come back to us safely.'

The spies were away for forty days, and in that time they travelled from end to end of Canaan and found out everything there was to find out about it. At the end of their journey they found a fertile valley full of fruits and they loaded up poles with great hanging wreaths of grapes, figs, and pomegranates, which they brought back on their shoulders to the waiting Israelites. The children and younger people had never seen fruit like this before, and the older ones sobbed with the memory of them, the taste and the smell of the rich sweet juices.

'The land is flowing with milk and honey,' the spies told Moses. 'It is wonderful.'

'Then we will enter, because it's truly ours,' he said. 'We have come to the end of our journey.'

But instead of rejoicing, the spies were afraid. After so many years of wandering in the desert, they didn't know how to fight or invade, and one by one they stood up and told the Israelites that it was better not to try.

'The walls are so high, we couldn't even scale them,' said Shammua.

'The people are so strong, we couldn't even fight them,' said Shaphar.

Caleb stood up and looked round at his fellow spies, amazed at their stories. 'It's not true. We are well able to occupy their land. There are hundreds of thousands of us. I think we should go in at once.'

The other spies groaned and shook their heads.

'You should see them! They're giants!' said Igal.

'It's true!' Palti agreed. 'Next to them, we're tiny grasshoppers. If one of them picked me up, I'd fit in the palm of his hand.'

'He'd close up his fist and crush you,' said Gaddiel. 'Or me, or any of us.'

And Gaddi rolled his eyes and sighed. 'No, I'm not going in there again. Not even for a basket of figs.'

The listening Israelites moaned with fear and turned on Moses. 'Why have you brought us here to die?' they asked. 'Why didn't you leave us in Egypt?'

But Caleb stood up again and silenced them. 'Believe me,' he shouted. 'These others are lying. Canaan will be easy for us to take.'

At last one of the other spies, Joshua, went to stand by his side. 'What Caleb says is true,' he said. 'Canaan is a rich and fertile land, the land of milk and honey. It is the land God promised us. We *must* take it.'

Both men tore off their clothes and stood naked in front of Moses and Aaron to show how honest they were, and how sincere their words were. But the Israelites were still afraid, and began to throw stones at them.

'You would lead us to death!' they shouted. 'You deserve to die yourselves.'

Enough! said God. He appeared among them like a golden light, and they all fell silent, wondering, shielding their eyes against the blinding light.

How long will my people despise me? God asked Moses.

I will strike them all dead

with pestilence and plague.

They have let me down.

They are not worthy of your leadership.

Moses begged God to spare them. 'If you strike them down now the Egyptians will get to hear of it. They will say you are not strong enough to lead us into the Promised Land,' he said. 'Remember the glory of the love you showed us in Egypt. Be merciful. Please, please forgive them.'

So, said God. *I will show mercy to some,*

but not to all. Their wickedness is too great.

Those Israelites who saw the wonders

I performed in Egypt and yet still refuse to believe in my love

will not enter the Promised Land.

Only the little children will be spared.

Only the tribes of Caleb and Joshua will be spared.

All the rest will die here in the wilderness.

Their children will wander for forty more years

because of the forty days

that were spent in the land of milk and honey.

And then, you will die here.

That is your punishment:

that is my word.'

It is said that fourteen thousand seven hundred Israelites died of the plague in the wilderness. God allowed Aaron to put an end to it by making a censer of holy incense. He stood between the dead and the living, and the sweet smoke drifted round them and the plague was stopped. It was soon afterwards that Aaron himself died, on Mount Hor. He was one hundred and twenty-three years old, and it was forty years since he and Moses had led the Israelites out of Egypt. Miriam had already died. It was truly time to end the wandering.

Moses was now one hundred and twenty years old, but old and frail though he was, weary with wandering, he climbed Mount Nebo alone. From there he could see all the land that was spread around him, all the blue rivers and golden pastures of Canaan.

In the middle of it all lay Jericho, the beautiful city of palm trees. And God said to him,

This is the Promised Land.

This I promised to Abraham,

to Isaac, to Jacob,

whose children have multiplied like stars in the sky,

like sand on the shore.

This is the land of milk and honey.

This land is for the Israelites.

Moses sank onto his knees. 'We are blessed,' he said. 'We have reached our home.'

But God said,

But not for you, Moses.

You have seen my face,

you have heard my voice,

you have brought terror and wonder

upon the people of Egypt.

You have freed the slaves.

You are the greatest of all my prophets.

Then Moses understood that his work was done. He closed his eyes and thanked God for the great power he had given him, for the gift of miracles and leadership. And there on Mount Nebo, high above the Promised Land, he gave up his ghost to God.

Joshua

So it was not Moses, but Joshua, who led the Israelites into the land of milk and honey. The greatest prize of all was the beautiful city of Jericho, which was thousands of years old. It was built on a fertile oasis in the scorching desert, and once Jericho was won, all Canaan would be won. But it would not be easy; it was surrounded by high, thick walls, guarded by soldiers. The people who lived in Jericho hated the Israelites; they would never let them take their city of palm trees away from them. But what they did not know was that if the Israelites did not enter by force, they could enter by the mysterious power of God.

The only thing that separated the Israelites from the land of Canaan was the River Jordan, deep and brown and washing its fertile banks like a rich flowing cloak. How were they to cross it, and how were they to bring the precious Ark of the Covenant to its new home? Wherever the Israelites went, the Ark of the Covenant must go. Joshua sent two men ahead as spies; they were to find the best place to cross the river, they were to enter the city of Jericho, they were to report back to Joshua about the mind of its citizens.

The men crossed the river by night and walked straight in through the gates of Jericho. At first they went unnoticed, but as soon as they were spotted a report was sent to the king that two Israelites were wandering his streets. He sent his soldiers to find them, to bring them to him, and to have them killed.

Joshua's two men had spent the night with a loose woman of the town, whose name was Rahab. Her house was built high up in the city walls, with a window facing away from the city towards the hills. At dawn Rahab heard the king's soldiers running down the street and banging on people's doors, shouting for the two Israelite spies to give themselves up.

'They're with Rahab,' she heard her neighbours saying. 'We saw them go into her house last night.'

'Quick,' Rahab shook the men awake and whispered urgently, 'run upstairs and onto the roof. I have some bundles of flax up there drying in the sun, hide yourselves inside them—quick quick, or we'll all be killed!'

Joshua's spies grabbed their clothes and ran upstairs, and Rahab went down to answer the soldiers at her door.

'People say you have two Israelites here,' the soldiers shouted.

Rahab lounged against the door, smiling at them sweetly. 'They came, yes, I don't deny it, I'm very popular. But I sent them away again,' she laughed. 'Whoever saw them coming should have seen them going, soldiers. The gates of the city were shut behind them as they left. I've no idea where they went then.'

The soldiers pushed past her and ran upstairs to search the rooms of her house, and on up to the roof. They gazed round them, but all they saw were bundles of flax, as yellow as the sun itself. If they had shoved them aside they would have seen Joshua's men crouching like street cats, hardly breathing, their eyes wide with fright.

'I told you,' Rahab said, standing with her arms akimbo and her loose red dress shifting in the early breeze. 'There's no Israelites here, soldiers.'

The king's men ran down the stairs and out through the city gates to search the fords and ditches surrounding the walls, and when the noise of their shouting had died down Rahab lifted the bundles of flax clear. 'I'll fetch a rope and lower you down the walls,' she told the spies. 'Run to the hills and hide there for a few days before you return to your people.'

'Thank you for saving our lives,' the men said, embracing her in turn.

'And I want you to save mine,' she said. 'When the Israelites have taken Jericho, as I know they surely will, I want you to spare me and my family.'

'We'll do that, as long as you tell no one where we are,' the men said. 'Tie red braid around your window, so our men will know you are to be spared. You keep your word, and we will keep ours. If any men harm you or your family, we will kill them.'

The men shinned quickly down the rope, and as soon as they were safely outside the walls of Jericho and running for the hills Rahab hauled the rope back inside and hid it, ready for her own escape when the time came. Then she tied the crimson braid to her window.

When the men returned to Joshua they told him how the people of Jericho lived in fear of the Israelites. 'They've heard how the Red Sea parted for us,' they told him. 'They've heard about our battles on the way here. They know we are coming for their city, and they are afraid.'

'Good,' said Joshua. 'Now, at last, the time has come.'

There was a rush of excitement in his voice, and the people heard it and sprang to their feet, ready at last for action. Forty thousand men followed Joshua to the banks of the river Jordan and stood in waiting lines, hungry to cross, hungry for the Promised Land. Joshua selected one man from each of the twelve tribes of the sons of Jacob, and they were to be the priests that would carry the Ark of the Covenant. Six men stood on either side of the ark and lifted it onto their shoulders, and stepped into the river. And as soon as their feet were in the water, it dried up in front of them, as if a dam had been built to stop the current flowing. The people of Jericho watched from the walls of their city and wrung their hands in fear.

The priests set off walking across the dry river bed, and when they came to the centre they lifted the Ark of the Covenant high, and Joshua led his forty thousand soldiers across to the other side. He told twelve men to lift twelve stones from the dry river bed and build a memorial on the other side, so the Israelites would always remember that the river Jordan had dried up to allow the Ark of the Covenant to be carried across. Another twelve stones were piled up in the centre of the river bed, and there they remain, even today.

As soon as the entire nation of Israelites had reached the other side, and the twelve priests lifted their feet onto the bank, the river flowed again. There on the banks, at a place called Gilgal, Joshua and his soldiers set up camp. They no longer needed the manna that God had sent them in the desert. They had no need of it ever again; they had the fruits and meats, the grains and the waters and the wines of their own country now.

But Jericho was still to be captured. As they approached the walls of the city, Joshua saw a man standing with a drawn sword in his hand. He approached him cautiously.

'Who are you, soldier?' he asked. 'Are you one of us, or one of our enemies?'

'Neither,' said the stranger. 'I lead the army of God.'

Joshua fell on his knees then. He took off his sandals and kissed the ground in front of the angel.

Now they were ready. Next day the Israelites advanced on Jericho. The priests led them, carrying high the precious Ark of the Covenant. They processed slowly and soundlessly towards Jericho, watched fearfully from the top of the city walls by the king and his advisers and captains. When they reached the walls they did not charge them, they made

no attempt to enter by force. They walked round the outside, a mighty river of men, in utter silence. They came again the next day, and the next, and did the same thing. For six days they made no sound, but walked slowly round the outside of the city carrying the golden Ark of the Covenant. The people of Jericho held their breath and waited. Nothing happened.

Then, on the seventh day, the Israelites walked six times round the city wall in silence, and on the seventh time they opened their throats and shouted, they banged their goatskin drums and timbrels, they blew their horn trumpets, they clashed their tambourines. And the walls of the city crashed down. Jericho was taken.

All the people who lived there, every man, woman, and child, was killed, except for Rahab and her family.

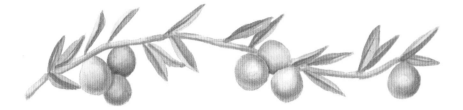

Gideon Against the Midianites

After Joshua died and was buried, the children of Israel turned back to their sinful ways. They forgot all about God, they forgot how Moses had led them out of slavery, and how Joshua had brought them into the Promised Land. They followed one false god after another. At last, to punish them, God gave them into the hands of the Midianites. For seven years the Israelites never knew a moment's peace. The Midianites destroyed or stole everything they had; they rode roughshod over their crops, they rustled their sheep and cows, even their donkeys. Their yellow camels strode across the fields like rolling waves of sand, there were so many of them. Their tents flapped like the wings of locusts.

It was hopeless. To save themselves, the Israelites had to desert their rich valley and live in caves. They grew what crops they could on the windy slopes of the mountains. Whatever they grew had to be stored away or the Midianites would have it all.

At last God took pity on the Israelites. He looked among them and chose a young man called Gideon to lead them, and then he sent an angel down to speak to him. Gideon knew nothing about soldiering and warfare; all he knew about was keeping himself and his father alive, and that was hard enough.

For a time the angel sat on a rock watching the young man grinding his meagre crop of wheat with a rough stone, and then he called out to him:

'Gideon, you are a mighty warrior. God is at your side.'

Gideon looked round, astonished. 'What do you mean? I'm not a warrior! I'm a farmer, or I'd like to be. And how can God be with me? God has left us!' He spread out his hands in despair.

'You will save your people,' the angel promised him. 'God will help you. But first, you must destroy the altar of Baal that you all worship at.'

His shadow grew tall, tall, taller than a tree, and then disappeared.

Gideon daren't touch the altar of Baal in the daytime. He knew that if he was seen, he would be stoned to death. He waited till dark and called ten men to go with him. They led his father's mightiest bull out of its enclosure and tied one end of a rope round the altar and the other end round the bull's neck. Then with sticks and whips they drove the bull home. Its muscles bulged, its eyes grew big, every fibre of its body strained, and at last the altar of Baal crashed to the ground and broke into hundreds of pieces. In its place Gideon built an altar to God, and sacrificed a second bull on it.

Next day, when the people of his town found out what he had done, they wanted to kill Gideon. His father was the only man to stand up for him.

'See what happens,' he told them. 'Let Baal take his own revenge, if that is what he wants.'

Before long the Midianites were gathering forces from all across the borders, bringing them over the river Jordan to fight the people who had destroyed Baal. They came in such vast numbers that they were a terrifying sight. Gideon begged for a sign that he was not alone, that God would help him.

'All I have is a fleece of a sheep,' he told God. 'I will leave it on the ground. Tonight the dew will come and soak everything. If tomorrow morning I find that the fleece is drenched, but all the ground around it is dry, I'll believe that you are there, and I'll have the courage to gather an army together.'

God was silent, but the next morning, sure enough, the fleece was drenched with dew, but the ground around it was dry.

'Please,' said Gideon. 'I just need one more sign. Can we do it again, but the other way round this time? Then I'll know for sure that you'll help me.'

So that night he left the fleece out again, but this time, when morning came, the fleece was bone dry even though the grass all around it was soaked with dew.

'Now we can fight the Midianites,' Gideon said. He called every man he could find to come with him. When they were all gathered together they were still far fewer than the Midianite army, but God said to Gideon, *There are too many. Send some away.*

'Too many!' Gideon exclaimed. 'But the Midianites have thousands more soldiers than we have.'

I say there are too many.

So Gideon turned and faced his band of men, the poor and the thin and the starving farmers who had agreed to fight with him against the Midianites.

'If any of you are afraid, go home,' he said.

Twenty-two thousand men put down their sticks and their swords and turned away to their mountain homes. Only ten thousand remained.

'This is my army,' said Gideon. 'They are all brave men, even though they are outnumbered.'

There are still too many, God said. *Send some away.*

So Gideon took the men to a spring that gushed out of the earth, and told them to drink. Some of them knelt by the spring and cupped the water in their hands to drink, and he sent these home. Some of them went on their hands and knees and put their faces into the water and lapped it up like a dog. Whenever he saw anyone doing this, Gideon put them to one side. When he counted them, he had three hundred men left.

They stood together looking at the colourful swarms of men in the valley below them, listening to the hubbub of their voices growling like thunder round the rocks.

If you are still afraid, listen to what they are saying, God said.

So during the night Gideon stole down towards the Midianite camp. He heard his name mentioned, and strained his ears to make out the words in the babble of voices.

'Gideon has the sword of God in his hand,' he heard. 'We are lost.'

Gideon ran straight back to his camp and woke up his men. 'We are victorious!' he told them. 'Do as I say, and we three hundred will overcome their three hundred thousand.'

Dazed, his men stood together with their swords in their hands. 'For God and for Gideon!' they shouted, eager to do what had to be done, believing in Gideon as they had believed in no other man.

He gave each of them a trumpet, a flaming torch, and a jar made of pottery. 'Cover the flame with the jar,' he told them. 'But don't smother it. Keep it alive, and follow me.'

He led them down to the valley, where all the Midianites were sleeping in darkness. He and his men spread themselves out silently, until they were surrounding the valley floor. Then, at Gideon's signal, they put their trumpets to their mouths and blew a shrill and fiendish blast. They smashed their jars so the torch flames blazed, and they roared, 'For God and for Gideon!' at the tops of their voices.

The Midianite army woke up in terror and confusion. They pulled out their swords and ran this way and that, charging into each other in the darkness, trampling each other in their haste to get away, crushing each other to death.

And so it was that Gideon overcame the Midianites, and not a single one of his three hundred men was hurt.

Jephtha's Daughter

Even after the Midianites were defeated, there was no peace for the Israelites. Their enemies swarmed round like wasps, plotting their revenge. The people were hated for what they had done. And it was a child who saved the Israelites from death and destruction.

She was the only daughter of a soldier called Jephtha. He was a captain in the Israelite army and led them to win many battles, but he was forced to leave home by his brothers, who hated him. They chased him away from Canaan, and he became an outlaw, well known for his fighting skills. Then he married a farmer's daughter and his life changed completely. He stopped fighting, he stopped running and hiding from the law. When his wife gave birth he felt that he was the happiest man on earth. He had a home, a wife who loved him, and a beautiful daughter.

Far away from there the Israelites were still fighting and being invaded. Their main threat at the time was the Ammonite army, and when they took Canaan by force Jephtha was summoned to fight for his old country. He didn't want to—why should he care about the Israelites, when they did not care for him? He wanted to stay with his wife and daughter, peacefully looking after his crops and his home. But he was offered the post of commander of all the forces of Israel, and so he accepted.

'I'll be back soon,' he promised his daughter when he kissed her goodbye. 'When I come home, we'll think of looking for a husband for you.'

She laughed. 'I'm too young for a husband!' she protested. But secretly she was excited at the thought. Some of her older friends were already making preparations for marriage; it wouldn't be long before it was her turn. Jephtha watched her as she danced away from him, waving and smiling; then she turned and ran to tell her friends what he had said.

He sighed and turned his horse towards Canaan. Already his mind was turning towards the task of soldiering, and that image of his child skipping away from him in her white dress floated in and out of his thoughts like a dream. 'I'll never go away to war again,' he promised himself.

The Israelites were waiting for Jephtha's arrival before they attempted to overthrow the Ammonites. He prepared his army for battle, but first he sent a warning to the king of the Ammonites, demanding that he remove his troops from Canaan. The king refused. There was nothing for it but for Jephtha to take his troops in and take it back by force. But Jephtha yearned to be home again, he wanted the battle to be quick and decisive. And so he made a bargain with God.

'Grant me victory today, and I will give you anything you ask for,' he said.

God was silent, and Jephtha spoke again.

'God, this is my promise. If my army wins, I will make you a sacrifice of the first living thing I see on my return home.'

Jephtha was a great soldier, and a great leader. The battle was short. The Israelites won, and the Ammonite army retreated from Canaan, carrying their dead and their wounded soldiers across the backs of their horses. Thankfully Jephtha turned his back on it all, all the bloodshed and agony, and rode home. He was free of all that now, free of the Israelites, free of soldiering and warfare. The battle had been swift and brilliant, but there would be no more, he was sure of that. There comes a time in every soldier's life when the killing has to stop. Now he would retire and live life as he wanted to, in peace with his family. His horse cantered across the desert, carrying him home.

Jephtha's daughter saw him coming before anyone else did. She had been watching out for him every day since he left, and now with a shout of joy she picked up her timbrel and went dancing across the sand to meet him.

'You're home, you're home. You're home at last!' she sang.

When Jephtha saw her coming, when he heard her voice and saw her dancing in the sand to meet him, he turned the head of his horse quickly; but he was too late. There she was, his daughter, his only child, laughing and running with her arms spread wide to greet him. Jephtha was beside himself with grief. He tried to rip the clothes from his body. He covered his face with his hands and wept.

'Why are you crying?' she asked him.

'Why, oh, why did you come to meet me?' he sobbed.

She gazed at him, not understanding why he was behaving like this, why he didn't jump down from his horse and wrap his arms round her and tell her how happy he was to see her again. 'Did you lose the war?' she asked hesitantly.

'No, we won the war.'

'Then why are you crying?'

'I won the war because I made a bargain with God. But I don't want to keep it.'

'Of course you must keep it. A promise is a promise. You've always told me that,' she said. 'What was your promise?'

But he couldn't tell her. 'Why, oh, why did you come running to me like that? Why couldn't it have been the chickens, or the dogs, or a goat? Why did it have to be you?'

'What was your promise? Tell me!' She shook the bells of her timbrel, trying to tease him out of his strange mood.

And at last he told her, and his voice was hollow with grief. 'My promise was that I would sacrifice the first living thing I saw on my return home.'

It was as if the sun had drained from the sky and would never be seen again.

'Not me,' his daughter whispered. 'Please, not me. Oh, please, not me.'

At last Jephtha dismounted. He put his arms round her and rocked her. 'You,' he whispered. 'It has to be you.'

Then she knew by his grief that it was true, that it was going to happen, and that there was nothing he or she could do about it, because a promise had been made to God, and a promise to God must be kept.

'Please let me live a little longer, to be with my friends, to be happy.'

He gave his daughter her wish. She turned away from him and went

to her friends, and they went with her up to the mountains. They cried with her, and for two months she stayed with them. One night she lay awake watching the stars and thought about the great happiness that life had given her, and how she must leave it for ever.

'I will never know what it means to love a man, to be his wife and have his children. That is what I wanted most, when I grow up, and now it will never happen. Now I will never grow up.'

All round her she heard the soft winds whispering of the promise that her father had made to God, and she tried to make sense of it all, to understand what had happened and what was going to happen.

'What do I care about the Israelites?' she wondered aloud. 'They mean nothing at all to me. But my father went into battle to save them. He risked his life for them. He made a promise to God so he could save them.'

One of her friends heard her and put her arms round her. 'You don't have to do it. You could run away,' she suggested. 'You could hide. We'd help you.'

Jephtha's daughter wrestled with this temptation. She could run until she came to another country, just as her father had done before she was born. She might meet a boy who wanted to save her, who would marry her and look after her. Surely she could do that?

'But what will happen to the Israelites, if my father breaks his promise? They are a great people, and I'm only a child. They are thousands of people, thousands of children. They must be more important to God than I am. They are worth a sacrifice. It is an honour to be that sacrifice.'

She was calm again now. When the first of the stars began to break in the sky, she went back down the mountain to her father's house.

'Father, we must keep your promise,' she said. 'I'm ready.'

Her courage gave Jephtha the strength to do what he had promised

God he would do. She dressed herself in the white dress that Jephtha loved to see her in, and went with him and lay on the altar stone and closed her eyes.

God accepted the sacrifice of Jephtha's daughter. But the sky wept all night, and the flowers that bloomed in the desert were as red as blood.

Samson, the Strongest Man in the World

Now, the most famous ruler of all was Samson, and he was the strongest man in the world.

His mother was a poor woman. She was working alone in the fields one day when she felt a breeze like a warm soft breath around her, and she heard the voice of an angel.

'You are going to have a baby.'

'A baby! But I'm barren,' the woman whispered, breathless with wonder.

'One day he will be a great leader. All men will bend in fear at his name. He will bring the Philistines down. But look after his hair for no one must cut it away.'

And it was true; she found that she was expecting a baby. He was a boy, and she called him Samson. His hair grew thick and long, and she plaited it into seven braids. Samson was stronger than any child that ever lived, and everybody was afraid of him because his will was as strong as his arms. If he was angry he would break anything that was near him, just by touching it. Whatever he ordered had to be done, immediately. Whatever he wanted had to be given to him. Yet when he loved, he loved with all his heart. That was his weakness.

So, when he was growing up, what should he do but fall in love with a Philistine girl, of all people.

'A Philistine!' his mother said, as he mooned round the house. 'Why does she have to be a Philistine! Think of all the lovely Israelite girls there are! You could have any of them!'

'I want her!' he shouted. 'Bring her to me!'

'But the Philistines are our enemies!' his father said.

'Get her!' Samson roared. 'I want to marry her. Now!'

The Philistines were a rich and powerful nation who had taken all the land and cities west of Judah as far as the Great Sea, and then advanced into central Canaan. They had dominance over all Israel and were hated and feared by all. What Samson was expecting of his father was beyond belief; he had to go into the Philistine town where the girl came from, find her father, and beg him to let her marry Samson.

'This will bring nothing but trouble,' Samson's father said, but because he loved his son and was frightened of his rages, he agreed to do it.

Samson went walking in the hills while he was waiting for his father to return, and he was attacked by a mountain lion. Now, everyone knows that it takes four to kill a lion: two to square him from behind, one to dance in front of him and distract him, and one to lunge in the knife. But Samson killed him on his own, tore the legs from the body, and ripped out the stomach with his bare hands. Then he tossed it to one side for the vultures to finish off.

His father came back with the good news that Samson could marry the Philistine girl, and he set off to her home for the wedding in Timnah. What should he see on the way but the stripped bones of the lion that he had killed. Bees had built a hive inside it. Brave, fearless Samson put both his hands into the hole where the lion's stomach had been, with bees humming and buzzing and lumbering round him, and pulled out the honeycomb. And ate it.

As well as being very brave, he was very boastful. At his wedding feast, when everyone was a little drunk and teasing one another with jokes and puzzles, he asked his Philistine guests a riddle.

'I bet you can't answer this. If you guess the answer in seven days, I'll give you a fine set of linen clothes,' he said. 'But if you can't, you have to give me a silk set.'

'So what's the riddle?' his guests asked, because they didn't have much choice in the matter.

Samson smiled. 'Out of the eater comes meat, and out of the strong comes sweet,' he said. 'What am I referring to?'

The guests looked at each other, puzzled. None of them had a clue what he was talking about. It annoyed them to think that an Israelite could defeat them in this way, and they were determined not to give in. They pestered his poor wife to give them the answer but she didn't have a clue, either. They teased her and flattered her and bullied her, and every night she begged Samson to tell her the answer to the riddle.

'No,' said Samson. 'Stop asking me.'

'Well, you don't love me,' she said on the seventh night, slyly plaiting his beautiful long hair round her wrists. 'If you really loved me, you'd tell me.'

And because his only weakness was love, he gave in and told her.

Of course, the first thing she did was to run laughing to the wedding guests and tell them the answer to the riddle, and they came knocking at his door first thing, full of triumph.

'Strength and sweetness, lions and honey,' they chanted. 'Honey came out of the belly of the lion that you killed. Give us our prizes, Samson.'

Samson was furious. 'You've been scheming with my wife to find this out!' he roared. He had been made to look a fool, and it was more than he could bear. He killed thirty of his wife's friends as a punishment to her, and then he left her. She had deceived him, and he told her he could never forgive her for that.

But before long he was sick with love for her again. He had to have her back. He bought her presents and went to Timnah to tell her that he had forgiven her and that he still loved her. Her father had no intention of letting this violent son-in-law anywhere near his daughter again, and told him that the marriage was over and that she had a new husband now. Samson's fury doubled and trebled. He tied flaming torches to foxes' tails and set the creatures loose in the wheatfields, and all the crops for miles around were burnt to the ground. When the farmers came searching for them he clubbed them to death with a donkey's jawbone. Then he ran away like a wild beast and hid in a cave.

Now all the Philistines in the area plotted to capture Samson and punish him. He lay in hiding, and would have died of thirst up in the mountains, but he prayed to God to help him.

'You have given me this power,' he said. 'Will you let me die before I have a chance to use it against the enemies of our people?'

A spring of water gushed up from the dry earth. Samson cupped it in his hands and drank his fill, and was well enough to go home. He became the leader of the Israelite people in his part of Canaan, and they called him their Judge. But all this time, years after the marriage to the girl of Timnah, the Philistines tried to capture him and punish him for what he had done. And one day, they had their chance.

Samson happened to come alone into the city of Gaza to visit a woman there. While he was in her house the Philistines surrounded it. They closed the gates of the city and set up guards on the walls. They were sure that this time, they would have him. But they hadn't bargained for his enormous strength. When he came out of the house and saw the Philistine officers waiting for him he barged through the crowd, pushing the men this way and that way as if they were dolls. Then he ran to the city gates, lifted them up on his shoulders, and ran away, laughing, wild and free.

Everyone was afraid of him, and everyone was fascinated by him. He looked the same as any other man, no taller or fatter or heavier, yet he had the strength of ten. What was his secret, everyone wanted to know. How could they tame him and make him just like one of them?

Perhaps no one would ever have found out if he hadn't happened to fall in love again. The name of his beloved was Delilah, another Philistine woman, and she lived in the valley of Sorek, near to the village where Samson was born. She of course was charmed and flattered to be loved by the strongest man in the world. But she proved to be as false to him as his first wife had been.

When the Philistine princes heard that Samson was visiting Delilah they went to her house and told her that it was her duty to tell them everything she knew about Samson.

'We must find out the secret of his strength,' they told her, 'otherwise there can be no taming or capturing of him. He's a danger to us all, Delilah.'

At first she refused to help them, but they each offered her eleven hundred pieces of silver if she would find out the secret of Samson's strength.

'Oh yes, I'll find out,' she promised immediately. 'Samson tells me everything.'

So that night she combed his lovely long hair, and she said, 'You're so strong, my love. If I wanted to capture you, how would I do it?'

'You've already captured me,' he teased her. 'But if you wanted to make sure I never got away, you would have to tie new bowstrings round me. I'd be helpless then.'

She kissed him and wound seven new bowstrings round him, just as he had said, tying the knots firmly behind his wrists and his knees and ankles. The Philistine lords were in the next room, listening and waiting, and at her signal they barged through the door. She didn't want him to know that she had betrayed him, so she shouted, 'Samson! Quick! The Philistines are coming to capture you!'

He snapped the bowstrings as though they were straws, tossed the lords aside, and escaped.

The next night she tried again, plaiting his lovely long hair and singing to him. 'You didn't tell me the truth about the bowstrings, did you? Now I'll never be able to capture you.'

'Try using ropes made out of green rushes,' he smiled. 'That would work.'

So she gathered green rushes and plaited them into a rope, just like his hair, and wound it round and round him, tight round his arms and chest, tight round his knees, tight round his ankles, while the Philistine lords waited silently in the next room.

'Oh, Samson, they're coming again!' Delilah shouted as the Philistines burst through the door, and he stood up and shook away the green ropes as if they were blades of grass, and sent the lords flying.

'Samson,' Delilah said on the third night, threading golden strands through his lovely long hair. 'Samson, you say you love me, but you never tell me the truth.'

'Yes, I do,' he said. 'This is the truth: weave my hair into your loom, and I'll never get away from you.'

He lay down on the floor and spread out the long black braids of his hair across her loom, and she threaded strands of gold and blue and red around them and pushed on her loom, pulled on her loom, pushed and pulled and sang, weaving a carpet of coloured threads and dark hair. But as soon as the Philistine lords burst into the room, up he sprang and snapped the threads as if they were strands of a spider's web, and shook his hair free.

The Philistine lords fled in fright, but the next day they crept back to Delilah, holding out more and more pieces of bright silver to tempt her.

'You must find out his weakness,' they said. 'He's a terror to us all. We must capture him. And when we do, all this silver will be yours.'

Well, she didn't give up then. She pestered and pestered Samson until he was sick to death of her questioning.

'No more questions!' he shouted. 'I've had enough of this!'

But Delilah was a cunning woman. 'Then you don't love me, Samson,' she wept. 'If you loved me, if you loved me true, you'd tell me how I can capture you.'

His heart melted with love. He held her in his arms and whispered to her. 'My strength is in my hair. If you cut it off, I'm yours.'

And she knew that this was the real answer.

She did nothing at first, just stroked his hair as he lay with his head in her lap. But as soon as he was asleep, she slid a small blade from under her cushion. Slish! she went, slicing through one of the braids. Slash! She sliced another. Seven times for seven braids, and singing all the time.

When the Philistine lords burst through the door Samson sprang to his feet and knew immediately that his strength had gone, that God had left him. He was no stronger than any other man. The Philistines overpowered him easily. They gouged out his eyes and threw him into prison.

And there he would have pined away in darkness, in shame, and in misery, but his hair began to grow again.

When the Philistines realized this, they wondered whether they should cut his hair off again. Then they decided that there was no point. He was now their prisoner; they could have a bit of fun with him. He could amuse the crowds, they decided, with his feats of strength. Everyone would come to see Samson, the lion turned lamb. Everyone would be fascinated to see whether his famous strength was really coming back.

They tied him up and dragged him into the temple of Dagon the fish-god, just outside Gaza. It was a massive temple which could hold thousands of people, and the Philistine lords travelled there from miles around to watch the spectacle. Townspeople scrambled up onto the rooftop of the temple, cheering as the rolling chariots flashed in the sunlight.

Samson could see nothing, but he could hear the shouts and laughter, the mockery of the people who had made him blind. They were the enemies of his people the Israelites. Well, he thought, they will have their show, but it will be the last time I will perform for them. He struggled to his feet and stretched out his arms. There was a hush of waiting. The Philistines craned their necks to see what Samson was going to do.

For a moment he did nothing, just stood with his arms stretched to either side, his hands resting on two of the massive pillars that held up the temple. He prayed to God for strength.

And then he pushed.

The great pillars cracked with a sickening shudder. The walls of the temple swayed and bulged, and then the mighty building cascaded to the ground, and all the people went with it, all the Philistine lords, all the men and women from the town, all were killed.

And Samson, the strongest man who had ever lived, was killed with them.

Ruth

Ruth lived with her parents in the country of Moab. One day when she was helping her mother to make bread she saw a Judaean family, strangers to her country, trudging along with a few bundles of belongings. They were obviously poor and hungry, and her mother told her to take them some food. Ruth was shy about doing this as she wasn't used to strangers. Besides, there were two boys in the family, and one of them was about her age. She gave them the food and left at once, embarrassed because the younger boy kept looking at her and smiling.

She soon found out that his name was Mahlon, and he made a point of finding out that her name was Ruth. It was not long before they fell in love, and Mahlon asked her to marry him.

Ruth's mother-in-law, Naomi, welcomed her lovingly into the household, and treated her as if she were her own daughter. Before long Mahlon's brother fell in love too, and soon Ruth had a sister-in-law, Orpah. They lived together and worked together, and they were a very close family, Naomi and Elimelech, Ruth and Mahlon, Orpah and Chilion. Ruth's own family lived nearby and she visited them whenever she could.

'Are you happy?' her mother asked her anxiously, and Ruth always laughed and replied, 'Yes. I live in a beautiful country, I love my husband, and I have two families. What more could I ask for?'

When Ruth and Orpah were helping Naomi to prepare food or to sew garments, the older woman told stories about the house and fields she and Elimelech had left behind in Bethlehem.

'What is it like, Bethlehem?' Ruth asked, and Naomi sighed.

'It is very beautiful. I would rather be there than anywhere, but we had a terrible famine. Can you imagine it—all the crops died. We had nothing. We walked here, all round the shores of the Dead Sea, over fifty miles we walked. And if it hadn't been for you and your mother, Ruth, I would have walked all the way back again, I was so homesick. But I'm happy here, now. We're all happy.'

But the happiness was short-lived. Tragedy struck the family. Naomi's husband, Elimelech, died, and then both his sons, Mahlon and Chilion. The three women had become widows. It was a terrible time for all of them, but it was worst of all for Naomi: she had lost her husband and her two sons. She felt as if her world had come to an end, and that there was nothing to live for. Ruth and Orpah did what they could to console her, but they were grieving too. Their husbands had died, they were penniless, and they had no one to turn to.

'You must go home,' Naomi told them. 'And so must I. This is not my home. My people are in Bethlehem, and I need them now. You two can return to your own families. I'm too old to marry again, but there's time for you, young and fit as you are. Fine-looking, both of you. You will find new husbands among your own people, and that's right. I'm sorry to let you go, but I need my own people.'

Sadly, Orpah did as Naomi told her. She hugged Naomi and Ruth goodbye, knowing that she would never see them again. 'You've been like a mother and sister to me,' she said. 'I'll always remember you.'

They watched her go, and then Naomi handed Ruth her bundle of clothes. 'Go quickly,' she said, 'back to your home like Orpah.'

But Ruth looked across the wide valley to where her old home lay, and turned back to Naomi.

'Naomi, I'm not leaving you.'

'You can't come with me,' Naomi said. 'You have your own family, and you'll be better off with them. Go, Ruth. I'll be all right.'

'How can I let you walk fifty miles all on your own?' Ruth asked. 'I want to stay with you, Naomi. Wherever your home is, will be my home too. Where you live, I will live. Where you die, I will die. Your people will be my people, and your God will be my God.'

So they went together to Bethlehem. Naomi had been right to go back; people recognized her as soon as they arrived, and they clamoured round her, welcoming her. When they heard that she had lost her husband and her sons, they promised her they would do what they could to help her set up her home again. She was among friends, and she was happy, but Ruth shrank into herself, lonely and shy among all these strangers, longing to be home again.

Although Naomi still had a house in Bethlehem, she had nothing else. She had no money or possessions, no animals. The fields that her husband had owned were on worthless, scrubby land; nothing grew there; never did, never would. If she managed to sell them she would have a little money, but who would want to buy them?

'Now you see why I wanted you to stay in Moab, Ruth,' she said. 'We have nothing. We'll starve, you and me together.'

But Ruth had no intention of letting either of them starve. It was the beginning of the barley harvest, and she went into the fields and walked behind the reapers as they gathered in the sheaves of grain. As she followed them she picked up every grain they had dropped. She worked all day without stopping for food or water. She was too shy and proud to ask for any, even when the reapers stopped for rest and food. At the end of the day the owner of the field, a wealthy man called Boaz, came down to see how the work was progressing. He watched Ruth following his reapers, knowing he had never seen her or anyone like her in his fields before. She was much taller and darker than the local girls, but there was something else about her that attracted him. She was modest and shy; she

looked at no one while she worked. But every now and again she would stand up and straighten up her aching back and she would gaze sadly into the distance.

'Who is she?' he asked his steward. 'Is she a foreigner?'

'She's a poor Moabite girl,' the steward said. 'She was married to Elimelech's son, but he died.'

'Elimelech? He was a cousin of mine,' Boaz said. 'So why is she grovelling like that in my field?'

'She asked permission to follow the reapers and glean, and I felt sorry for her,' the steward said.

'You did right,' said Boaz. He couldn't take his eyes off Ruth now. He noticed how sad and lonely she looked, and he wondered what it must be like for her, a stranger in a foreign land, poor and longing for home. His heart went out to her. 'Let her follow the reapers, and tell them that they must drop a handful from time to time for her to find. Tell the men to leave her alone—if anyone touches her he will be punished.'

Then he took a pitcher of water and went over to Ruth and gave it to her. 'Drink,' he said. 'You must be weak with thirst. If you need bread, go and eat with the other girls.'

When he approached her she had lowered her eyes, afraid that he was going to shout at her and send her away, even though it was a rule in Bethlehem that the very poor could do as she was doing at harvest time. He spoke so gently to her that she dared to speak to him.

'I hope you don't mind,' she said, showing him her basket with its few handfuls of barley grains.

'You are welcome. I've heard of the great kindness you've shown to my cousin's widow, Naomi,' he said, and she looked at him at last and saw how warm his eyes were, and how gently he smiled at her. 'Don't go into any of the other fields,' he said. 'Stay in mine.'

And so she went back there every day of the barley harvest, and then during the wheat harvest that followed. When the other reapers were having their meal Boaz stood watching her, and he brought her water and a little bread, and after a while he lingered a little, just in the hope that she would smile at him, and she sometimes did. She found herself watching out for him from time to time, though when he arrived she would stoop to her task and pretend not to notice him.

Soon the house where Naomi and Ruth lived had its store of grains. The days were changing, the harvests would be over soon, but there would be enough to keep them alive during the winter. Ruth came home at night weary from so much bending and walking, but full of chatter about how kind Boaz was to her, and Naomi was old enough and wise enough to notice how the girl blushed when she talked about him, and to know what this meant.

One evening when a soft wind was blowing from the hills Naomi stood at the door of the house and said, 'I think it is time for you to go to Boaz, Ruth.'

'Why?' Ruth asked, startled. Surely if anyone should go to him, it should be Naomi, because he was her husband's cousin after all. And if she went to him, what should she say?

'Why?' Naomi smiled and deliberately misunderstood her. 'Because tonight he is in the threshing barns winnowing the wheat, and this wind is so soft and so perfect that he will be working all night with his threshers, good man that he is. And he will sleep there so he can begin again at dawn. He will be lying apart from the others. This is what you must do, Ruth. Go to him tonight. Uncover his feet as he sleeps, and lie there, and he will tell you what to do.'

She put her arms round her daughter-in-law and hugged her. 'You are so good to me, Ruth. I loved you the moment my son asked you to be his wife. I am asking a great deal of you, but can you bring it into your heart to love a man who is old enough to be your father?'

'I can,' Ruth whispered, and wrapped her shawl round her and ran down to the threshing barns while it was still light enough to see.

Under the canopy of the barns the threshers were beating the sheaves of wheat. The breeze took the chaff and floated it in the air, while the heavier grains fell to the ground. The air was dusty with the winnowed chaff, and golden with the light of the setting sun. Ruth could see Boaz at the far end, working as hard as his men, and she thought, how good he is, how kind and diligent.

When the stars were up and the night was thick the workers took their rugs and blankets and went outside to snatch a few hours' sleep before dawn. Ruth watched Boaz and saw that he went to sleep apart from the others, just as Naomi had said he would. He lay on the ground, pulled his rugs round himself, and fell asleep straight away; the sleep of the weary. Ruth approached him nervously. Would he be angry at her boldness? she wondered. How shameful it would be if he sent her away. And yet it would help Naomi so much if she could be brought back into the wealthy family of her husband's cousin.

So she crept up to Boaz and lifted away the blanket that covered his feet, and lay there, a little afraid, a little excited to be so near him. The coldness soon woke him, and as he sat up to cover his feet, he saw her there.

'Ruth,' he said. 'Why have you come to me like this?'

'Because I wish to,' she said.

'You could have gone to any young man in Bethlehem, and yet you came to me. I'm so glad. But you must know that I don't have the right to cover us both with my blanket and take you in my arms, much as I want to. It is a cousin's right, but Elimelech had a cousin who is closer to you than I am. His right is greater than mine. Did you know this?'

'No,' Ruth faltered. Would Boaz send her away again? 'I came to you because Naomi told me to, and because . . . because you are such a good man. And because I wanted to,' she whispered.

'Stay at my feet,' Boaz said. Even in the dark she could tell that he was smiling. 'But go before dawn, so no one knows you have been here. I'll see what I can do.'

So Ruth stayed curled up at his feet, keeping him warm, but she didn't sleep. She stared into the darkness and wondered what would become of her now. Must she marry this other cousin, a man she didn't even know?

And Boaz lay with his eyes closed, but he didn't sleep either. Now that he knew that Ruth loved him as much as he loved her, must he give her up to another man?

Just as grey light was stealing into the sky he felt a slight movement at his feet, and he knew that Ruth had slipped silently away. He sent his steward to Naomi's house with a present of barley, and she smiled at Ruth.

'This is to show that Boaz is thinking of me, and he's thinking of you,' she told her. 'Be patient, child. Before the day is over he'll have decided what to do.'

That evening, when the winnowing was over, Boaz went to the elders of Bethlehem and asked them to sit with him at the gates of the town, so they could be witness to what he was about to do. Soon a man passed by, a man full of importance and fuss, and Boaz hailed him. This man was the first cousin of Elimelech. He was a blustery, busy man, who really did not have time to spend with Boaz, even though they were related in a distant way.

'Sit with us for a moment,' Boaz called. 'I want to speak to you about Elimelech's widow, Naomi.'

'What about her?' the cousin asked. 'She's as poor as a mouse. Why didn't she stay in Moab?'

'This is her home,' Boaz reminded him gently. 'But you're right, she's as poor as a mouse. I've thought of a way you could help her. Elimelech had a couple of fields, which she can't use herself. As his first cousin, you have the right to buy them from her.'

The cousin snorted and shook his head at once. 'Nothing but scrubland, those fields. No, I'd be wasting my money to buy them.'

'Perhaps I should remind you that if you buy the fields, you have the right to marry her daughter-in-law. It's our law and custom.' He did not want to say this, but he had to. He was an honest man, though the thought of letting Ruth marry this uncaring man was very painful to him.

The cousin considered for a moment. He had noticed Ruth, and her calm, still beauty was attractive to him. But that scrubland would take his spare money away, and what use was it to him?

'No,' he said, shaking his head.

Boaz jumped up quickly before his cousin could change his mind. His face was bright with smiles.

'The elders are witness,' he said. 'You have relinquished your right to Naomi's land and Ruth's hand, so the right is passed on to me. Give me your sandal.'

The cousin took off his sandal, as is the custom, and gave it to Boaz in front of the elders to show that he gave up his rights, and Boaz could hardly conceal his happiness. He hurried straight to Ruth and asked her to marry him, and she, of course, said 'Yes'.

So it was that Ruth and Naomi entered the wealthy family of Boaz. It was a warm and loving household again, and they lived in comfort for the first time in their lives. A year later Ruth had a baby boy. It was the proudest moment of her life when she put him into Naomi's arms as if he were the old woman's own child.

And the boy was called Obed. He was to become the grandfather of David, and *he* was the ancestor of Jesus of Nazareth himself.

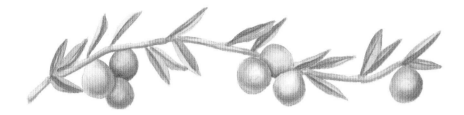

Samuel

It's not often that a child hears the voice of God, like a vision, but that is what happened to a boy called Samuel. He lived with a priest called Eli, and the only time he saw his mother, Hannah, was when she brought new clothes for him. She had given birth to him when she thought she was too old to have any children, and in return for this great blessing she had promised him to Eli. Eli's own sons were scoundrels who broke God's law, so the priest liked having Samuel in his care. Every day they walked together in the vineyards around Shiloh and Eli gave him lessons and talked to him about the laws of God. One day, he thought, Samuel would also be a priest. But God had even greater plans for him, and that was why he came to the boy in such a mysterious way. It was like this.

When the vision happened, there was actually nothing to see, only a voice in the darkness. Samuel was sleeping in the temple near Eli when he heard a voice calling to him:

Samuel! Samuel!

He woke at once, and thought it was Eli calling. 'I'm here,' he said. 'What do you need?'

'I didn't say anything,' said Eli. 'Go back to sleep.'

A bit later, he heard the voice again: *Samuel! Samuel!* and again he ran over to Eli and asked him what he wanted.

'Nothing,' Eli yawned. 'Go back to sleep, Samuel.'

It happened a third time, and Eli realized that the boy must be hearing the voice of God himself. 'If he calls you again, speak to him,' he said.

'What shall I say?'

Eli thought for a little. What should a boy say to God? 'Say, "Speak, your servant is listening." And tell me what he says, won't you?'

Samuel ran back to his roll of blankets and lay with his eyes wide open, staring at the flickering light of the temple lantern, and then, at last, he heard the voice again.

Samuel! Samuel!

'Speak, your servant is listening,' Samuel whispered, brave and excited and full of awe and trembling.

What I will tell you will make any man shake with fear.

It is about Eli.

His sons have sinned against me,

Eli has done nothing to stop them.

I will punish his house and his family

for ever.

The light of the lantern went out, and Samuel lay in the dark with the words swirling round his head like wild wolves. *I will punish his house and his family for ever.* How could he tell Eli this terrible thing? The next morning he ran to open the doors of the temple to let in the sunlight and the air. He wanted to chase away the words, he wanted to forget them, but Eli followed him.

'Tell me what God said to you.'

So Samuel told him everything. At first Eli was silent, and then he said:

'I believe what you say, because God has chosen you to be a prophet. And as for what you have told me, God must do what he thinks best.'

And this is how God's prophecy to Samuel came true: the Israelites suffered another defeat by the Philistines. Much worse was to happen. They decided to bring the Ark of the Covenant to Shiloh; it was their great comfort; whenever it was with them, they thought that God must be with them too. The Ark was carried into their camp and they gave such a huge shout of joy and relief that the earth and the mountains rang. The Philistines heard the shout, and were filled with fear. 'Their God is a terrible god,' they said. 'We must defeat them completely.'

They advanced into battle again, and this time, not only did they win, but they stole the Ark, the most precious thing that the Israelites owned, the earthly home of God himself. And when Eli heard the news, he died of a broken heart.

But the Ark of the Covenant did the Philistines no good. They brought it home and set it up in their temple of Dagon. Next day they found the golden statue of Dagon lying in pieces on the ground. They were horrified. They looked at one another, and found that they were all covered with painful red boils. A plague of rats scurried across their land, devouring their crops, ruining their stored food.

'The God of the Israelites is too powerful for us,' they told one another. 'We must get rid of it.' Fearfully, they loaded the Ark and a casket of gold onto a cart and put cows between the shafts. Without even a driver to lead them, the cows set off with their precious load, and took it all the way home to the people of Israel.

Saul

The Israelites were desperate to have a king who would unite the twelve tribes and rule them as one. Samuel told them that a bad king would be worse than no king at all: he would rule them like a tyrant, he would take their land and their goods and their women for his own. But they insisted that he should find them a king to protect them and lead them against the Philistines.

And then, one day, Samuel saw a young farmer's boy approaching him. The boy's name was Saul, and he had left home days before with his servant, searching for some donkeys that had strayed away. They had given up hope of finding them. In fact, they'd been away from home for so long that Saul thought his father would have stopped worrying about his donkeys and would be worrying about him and his servant instead.

'Let's go back,' he said, but his servant told him that the famous prophet Samuel was visiting the area.

'Perhaps he can help,' he suggested. 'If anyone knows where they are, Samuel does. He's supposed to know everything, isn't he?'

So that was why Saul was trudging along the dusty road towards the old prophet on that particular day. And as soon as Samuel saw him, he knew he had found the future king of Israel.

Anoint this boy, God said to him.

He is the one who will save my people from the Philistines.

'Your donkeys are safe,' Samuel said to Saul. 'Send your servant home, and come with me.'

He made Saul a special guest at a feast, and then he took him to a private place and anointed him with holy oil.

'God wants you to rule his people,' he said, and kissed him.

'How can I do that?' asked Saul. 'I don't know anything about ruling people. I only know how to look after donkeys, and I don't do that very well.'

'Later today you will meet a band of prophets returning from a religious festival,' Samuel said. 'They'll be very excited and full of holy happiness—they'll be singing and dancing and wild with joy. Join with them, do what they do, and it will change you into a different man.'

And that was what happened. When Saul returned home at last he felt he was a different person, almost as if his heart was stronger, but he said nothing of what had happened to him, or of how the famous prophet had told him he was to be king of all Israel.

Soon after this, Samuel called together all the tribes of Israel. They came from all parts, travelling on camels and horses and donkeys, to see whether he had done what they had asked him to do.

'I have led you since I was a boy,' Samuel said. 'My hair is grey now. I'm an old man, and you have asked for a new leader. Yes, I have done what you asked, I have found you a king. This is the man the Lord has chosen. His name is Saul.'

Everyone craned to have a look at their promised king, but Saul was hiding among the piles of baggage and had to be called for again before he emerged shyly to stand at Samuel's side.

'Look at him,' Samuel said. 'He stands head and shoulders above the rest of you. He is a man of men. Nobody else is like him.'

'Long live the King!' the cry went up.

So, the first king of Israel had been appointed. Not everyone was pleased, not everyone liked him, but because they trusted Samuel, they accepted the king he had found for them. But some years later, King Saul betrayed Samuel's trust, and once again he changed into a different person.

This is how it happened. King Saul had called together all his army to fight the Philistines. It was to be a huge battle. The Israelites were frightened because there were so few of them in comparison to the huge Philistine force. They waited for Samuel to come and make a sacrifice to help them succeed in the battle, but after seven days Samuel still hadn't come, and King Saul was impatient. His men were beginning to slip away, back to their homes and farms. It was time to fight.

'Bring me the burnt offering,' he said. 'I will make the sacrifice in Samuel's place to ask God's favour.'

And that is what he did, but as soon as the sacrifice had been made Samuel arrived.

'What have you done?' he demanded. 'You have broken God's commandment. You have lost his favour and mine. He thought you were a man after his own heart, your family would have been kings of Israel for ever. God will find someone else who will serve Him better, who will rule in your place.'

From that day, fear gripped King Saul. His heart was weaker, he was pursued by tormenting voices, and his life was changed for ever. He was always afraid now. Who would God send to replace him?

David the Giant-Killer

David was a poor shepherd boy who became a court minstrel, and then a giant-killer, and then an outlaw, and then the great king of the Israelites. How could all this happen? It was because God poured himself into the boy's heart, that's how, and this is the story.

When David was still a child and wandering the hills and fields around Bethlehem with his father's sheep, the king of the Hebrew tribes was Saul. But God was angry with Saul because he had disobeyed him. He told his prophet, Samuel, to go to Saul and tell him he must prepare for his downfall.

'God has rejected you,' Samuel told the king sadly. 'He does not want you to be king any more.'

God took his love away and poured the spirits of darkness into Saul's soul, and these spirits haunted him night and day, day and night, with a strange kind of madness. Saul knew that the prophet was his friend and adviser, and that what he said must be true. He was in a torment of despair, and the spirits nagged him with suspicions and fears, wondering who it might be who would overthrow him, and how it would be done.

Then God told Samuel to go and find the future king, and anoint him so he would be prepared for his duties when the time came.

'How will I know when I've found him?' Samuel asked.

You will know.

Go to Bethlehem and find a man called Jesse.

This man who is born to be king is one of his sons.

Look into his heart,
and you will know.
I do not see the outside of men,
I see into their hearts,
and so must you.

Samuel travelled to the little hill town of Bethlehem and asked to see Jesse. Jesse was surprised that this famous prophet had come to see him, and even more surprised when Samuel asked him to present his sons to him. Seven men came to Samuel, all tall and strong and fit, but as each one came forward and knelt in front of him Samuel shook his head.

'No, this is not the one, nor this, nor this, nor any of these seven. Are you sure these are your only sons?'

Jesse laughed. 'Well, I have another, but he's only a child, a simple shepherd boy. He'll be up in the hills somewhere, playing his flute to the sheep!'

'Bring him, all the same,' Samuel said.

So David was sent for, and he came running, shy and fresh and bright-eyed, with his wooden flute in his hand. He wore a loose shirt with one sleeve pulled away, and over his shoulder he had a leather thong with a pad for slinging stones. He looked wild and young, and there was nothing of the king about him at all, but Samuel looked into his heart and knew at once that he was the one.

'Come here, David,' he said. 'Kneel down. God has chosen you.'

David had no idea what this might mean, but he did as he was told. Samuel anointed him with olive oil perfumed with spices and myrrh, and at that moment David felt dignity and courage and wonder flowing through him.

'What does God want me to do?' he asked.

'You will find out,' Samuel promised him. 'When the time is right.'

David went back to tending his father's sheep, and forgot all about the strange visitor. When he was lonely he played music on his flute and made up songs about the wild beasts of the mountains, the lions and bears and wolves. Sometimes they attacked his sheep, and he would put a pebble into his sling and hurl it at them and kill them. Nothing frightened him, but then, he had no idea what the future held for him, or what it was that God wanted him to do. He might have been frightened if he had known.

Far away in his royal tent, King Saul was sick and wretched. He knew nothing of what had happened in Bethlehem, yet his dark spirits haunted his dreams and tormented his waking hours with uncontrollable fears. He was convinced that he was surrounded by unseen enemies. At times like this he lost his reason; he ranted like a madman, and people were afraid of him. His son, Jonathan, and daughters, Merab and Michal, watched him anxiously.

'Perhaps music would help to soothe him,' one of the servants said. 'I know of a shepherd boy in Bethlehem who is said to play and sing like an angel.'

'Yes, send for him. We'll try anything!' Jonathan said.

And, of course, that shepherd boy was David. When he was sent for he brought a harp that he had made himself, and he was afraid and proud to be asked to play for the king. The king lay alone. Every rustle of the flapping goatskins that covered the tent startled him, the flickering lamp brought lurking shadows. When David came in he sat up and screamed in terror, and David was just as afraid. Neither of them knew that one day David would be king instead of Saul. They were just a man and a boy, afraid of each other.

David took up his harp and began to play. His fingers were trembling as he stroked the strings, but he soon lost himself in his music. It was just as beautiful as the servant had said, and when he sang his voice was so sweet and pure that the king became calm again. He wanted David with him all the time; he made him his armour-bearer as well as his minstrel. And more than that, he began to love him and to think of him as a son. But David still thought of himself as a shepherd and he was homesick for his old life. As soon as the king was well enough David returned to Bethlehem, to the solitude of the hills, to the quiet night stars.

One day David heard that the Philistines had invaded Judah again. His seven brothers had been summoned to join the Israelite army to fight them. Thousands of soldiers were being called to the narrow valley to the west of Bethlehem where the battle was to take place. As he had been the king's armour-bearer David felt he ought to be there. He left the sheep in the care of his cousin and hurried to the place of battle. His father had given him gifts and food for his brothers, and he pushed his way through the throng of soldiers kitting themselves up in their battle armour. But when they saw him they tried to send him away.

'This is no place for a boy like you,' his older brother said. 'Get back to your sheep.'

It was then that David saw the giant.

His name was Goliath. He was the greatest soldier in the Philistine army, and he gleamed like a bronze god in his armour. The Philistine soldiers wore kilts and pleated head caps, but Goliath the giant was in full armour. He wore a helmet and silver chain-mail and breast-plate, huge shin-guards made of bronze, a mighty javelin slung across his back. Two armour-bearers carried his shield, which was as long as a chariot. Another two carried his massive tree of a spear. He strode towards the Israelite army, and every man there went silent, watching him and wondering. He stopped in the middle of the valley, where everyone could see him, and he sent his voice bellowing round the hills.

'Saul of the Hebrews, I challenge you to send one of your soldiers to fight me! Between us we will fight the war of the Philistines against the Israelites. If I win, you and your people will lose your land and be our slaves for ever, King Saul. But if your man wins, which he won't, we will plough your fields and build your homes and be your very humble servants.'

He roared with laughter, and King Saul's soldiers looked at one another in fear. To fight in an army was one thing; you might win or lose, but you had a chance. To fight single-handed against a giant was quite another. There was not a man among them who wasn't frightened to his very heart. No one spoke, but stood with eyes cast down, deeply afraid.

Then David knew what he had been chosen to do.

'I'll fight the giant,' he told King Saul.

The king shook his head. 'It's out of the question. You're only a boy. Goliath is the greatest warrior alive.'

'But let me try,' David begged. He looked round, opening his arms out to show that none of the other soldiers were offering. 'I'm not afraid of bears and lions—why should I be afraid of a giant?'

'You don't even have any armour!' the king said, but David shrugged. 'I'm not used to wearing armour. It would slow me down.'

He ran towards the giant.

'You don't have any weapons!' King Saul shouted in despair.

'Yes I have.' David stooped down by the bed of a dried-up river and

picked out five pebbles, and stood waiting.

The giant roared in anger. This was not a soldier in gleaming armour. This was just a barefoot boy in a shirt with a torn sleeve. Was he, the greatest warrior in the world, being mocked? Goliath should have known better. He should have been afraid of that bare right arm, but he was only a soldier, not a shepherd. He was only a giant, not a boy of the hills defending his flock. He did not know how to be afraid.

'Is this puppy the best you can find, Saul of the Hebrews?' he roared. 'I don't fight children! Get away, boy! The beasts of the desert will rip your flesh to shreds, the vultures of the air will tear you to pieces, when I have done with you!'

David placed the first pebble in the pad of his sling. 'I have killed lions, I have killed wolves,' he said quietly. 'Beware, giant Goliath. I have come to you in the name of the Lord. Today you will die.'

Goliath came lumbering across the valley floor towards David. His sword sliced the air. David lifted up his bare arm and swung the sling round and round his head, and the pebble flew. It struck Goliath in the middle of his forehead; one single blow, and he crashed like a mighty tree to the ground.

The giant was dead.

> *My heart is steady, O Lord,*
> *Steady is my heart.*
> *I will sing and make music*
> *Awake, my inspiration!*
> *Awake, harp; awake, flute and lyre*
> *I will wake up the day with song! ·*

MANY OF DAVID'S SONGS HAVE BEEN WRITTEN DOWN.
THIS ONE IS FROM PSALM 108.

David the Outlaw

David cut off Goliath's head and handed it to King Saul, and the king hugged and kissed him as if he were his own son.

'Stay here with me. I've missed your singing, and now I find you're a brave warrior as well as a musician. Stay with us. Don't go back to your father's house.'

'You're one of our family now,' Saul's son Jonathan said. He put his arm round David and led him away, and Saul watched them go, smiling. Yet something was worrying him.

'He's stealing your son away,' nagged the jealous spirits of darkness.

Jonathan loved David. He knew that David's music had saved his father's life, and now his bravery had saved the Israelites from Goliath and sent the Philistines fleeing in terror. As a token of his deep friendship he gave David his own robes and armour to wear, and suggested that David should be put in charge of Saul's entire army. It was a tremendous honour for a poor shepherd boy. David thought back to the day he had run in from the fields and met the great prophet Samuel, and how the old man had anointed him with holy oils. He remembered then the feeling of dignity and courage that had surged through him.

It seemed as if he could do nothing wrong. Under his leadership the army won every battle. People cheered him wherever he went because he freed them from their enemies and he made the Israelites great and powerful. When he led his victorious armies home, people rushed to greet him, they waved flags and banners, they danced and blew their horns and rattled their tambourines; and this is what they sang:

Saul kills thousands

But David kills tens of thousands!

Hooray for David!

Imagine how King Saul felt when he heard this. He was angry and jealous; he couldn't help it. Nobody had ever cheered *him* like this.

'He's stealing your followers away,' the spirits nagged him. 'You are the king, not David.'

Saul couldn't forget what the prophet Samuel had told him. God has rejected you, the old man had said. He does not want you to be king any more. That was how his feverish illness had started, and now it was beginning again, driving him mad with anger and suspicion and fear. Over and over churned the voices of the spirits of darkness:

'The people love David more than they love you. They will make him their king. God loves David more than he loves you. He wants David to be king.'

Saul fell into a fever and became ill again. He couldn't forget Samuel's warning: 'Prepare for your downfall, King Saul. God has chosen another to rule your kingdom.'

Who was this other person to be? And when would his downfall come? He tossed and turned on his bed, feverish with fear. Nothing that the physicians or magicians could do would help him.

Jonathan begged David to take his harp to the royal tent and play and sing to Saul as he used to do. David went gladly, but nothing could drown out the voices: Saul couldn't close his ears to them, he couldn't hide from them; they were inside his heart, winding in and out of the sweetness of David's singing, drowning the music. His heart was black with the thoughts, black with hatred and suspicion of David himself.

'Kill him! Kill him!' the voices chanted, and with a roar the king picked up his spear and flung it at David's heart.

David leapt out of the way just in time. He couldn't believe what was happening, that the king who loved him so much was trying to kill him. King Saul shuddered violently and shook the spirits away. He came out of his black mood as if he was waking up from a nightmare, and stared at David.

'Do you want me to go back to my father's home?' David asked.

'No, no, stay here. I want you here,' King Saul said. 'You are my son.'

So David stayed. But before long the king's loathing and fear rose up again. He watched David all the time. 'David is brave and beautiful. Everybody loves him,' the voices said.

'I hate him!' King Saul shouted.

'You must get rid of him.'

There was only one honourable way to get rid of a soldier. King Saul decided to send David into battle against the Philistines, but with such a small army behind him that he couldn't possibly survive. He watched David go bravely to his death, and sighed with relief. He was rid of him for ever.

But David did not die. He came back victorious, and all the people were wild with love for him.

'Saul kills thousands, but David kills tens of thousands!' they chanted. They flocked to meet him, thousands of people in all their brightly coloured robes, filling the air with cheers and singing. David was the greatest hero of all time.

'David, David!' they chanted wherever they went. 'David the brave! David the great! David the leader!'

'Listen to them! They want him to be king!' The spirits of darkness hissed into Saul's dreams. 'He will steal your kingdom away.'

King Saul knew that one day the Philistines would kill David. They had to; there were so many of them, and only one David. Saul only had to be patient, and it would happen.

'Stay with us, marry my daughter, Merab,' he said to David, calm with cunning. It would be a way of keeping David in his sight while he plotted what to do with him.

But David refused. 'I'm only a poor shepherd boy,' he said. 'How can I marry the daughter of a king?'

What David didn't say was that he didn't love Merab anyway, he loved King Saul's younger daughter, Michal. But the king was amazed that David had turned his offer down. He was even more afraid of him now. David had such courage and confidence; surely these were the qualities of a king. He had to love and admire David for everything he did, and yet he hated him for it.

'I will marry your younger daughter,' David said.

'Michal?' King Saul was puzzled that David would marry the younger daughter rather than the older. It wasn't the way things should happen. But he agreed to the wedding rather than lose David to somebody else. And when he saw David and Michal together, holding hands, gazing into each other's eyes, his jealousy rose up again. They were in love with each other. Marriage was one thing; it could be freely given. But love was quite another.

'He is stealing your daughter's love,' the spirits of darkness snarled. 'Kill him!'

Saul decided to act straight away, before he lost everything. He called his chief servant and ordered him to kill David. The servant was shocked. Everybody loved David, why would the king want to kill him? He went to Jonathan in secret and asked him what he should do.

'Leave it with me,' Jonathan said. 'I'll try to talk my father out of his madness.'

He went to the king and begged him to spare David's life.

'Think how good and brave he is,' he said. 'Think how everyone loves him. Remember how he killed the giant for us!'

'Of course, of course,' the king said. 'Don't worry, Jonathan. David is my son. Bring him to me and let him sing.'

Saul sat with his head in his hands, deeply troubled, trying to understand himself. One minute he hated David enough to kill him, the next minute he loved him like a son. How could he control these wild emotions? Maybe music would help.

But as soon as David had come and was playing his beautiful music, the spirits taunted Saul again.

'He steals your daughter, he steals your son, he steals your people, and he steals your God!' they chanted. 'Why should he live?'

King Saul flung his spear at David again, just missing him, and this time David fled for his life.

'Follow him!' the king shouted to his men, desperate now. 'Kill him!'

David ran to the house where he and Michal lived and bolted the door. He could hear the soldiers running up to the house. Now they were hammering on the door. He ran upstairs to hide, and Michal begged him to tell her what was happening.

'Why does your father hate me so much? He wants to kill me!' David told her. 'His men are breaking the door down now—listen to them!'

'Then you mustn't stay here. You must go, David. With all my heart I want you to stay here with me. But I know my father. He won't leave you alone now. Go, my beloved husband.'

She plaited sheets together and lowered David out of the back window, while round at the front of the house the king's followers tried to ram the door down. Michal put a statue in David's bed and covered it over with sheets, and waited, crying and shaking. The only thing she wanted was for David to be safe.

At last the men burst in and thundered up the stairs.

'Leave him, he's sleeping,' Michal begged, pointing to the bed. But the king's followers raised their clubs and hammered the statue to a thousand pieces.

And that is how David became an outlaw, hiding and hunted, away from his father and brothers and the farmland that he loved, away from Jonathan and Michal, homeless and destitute, always on the run, always looking to save his life. He was the bravest soldier who had ever lived, and now he was like a hare fleeing from the fox. And as he hid himself in caves and forests he came across other men who were hiding from the king, robbers and tricksters, thieves and vagabonds. They were a gang of wanted men and they roamed the wilderness, a terror to King Saul. David joined them. They were always on the run, David and the outlaws.

Then one day the chance came for David to take matters into his own hands. One of the outlaws saw that King Saul was nearby with his soldiers. He had gone on his own into a cave to take some rest.

'Go in and kill him,' the other outlaws urged David. 'Then you'll be free. We'll all be free.'

It was a great temptation. If Saul was dead, David would be able to stop running and hiding. He would be able to see Michal and Jonathan again. He would be able to visit his father and his brothers, he would have his old life back. He crept into the cave. There was the king, standing with his back to him. How easy it was going to be. He lifted his knife stealthily.

But David did not kill Saul. Instead he used his knife to cut off a tiny piece of the king's robe. Saul didn't see him or hear him; he knew nothing of what was happening. When he came out of the cave again, David was waiting for him.

'I could have killed you just now,' David said. He knelt down in front of the king and gave him the piece of cloth. 'Your life was in my hands.'

Amazed, the king looked down at his robe and saw how near to him David's knife had been. He broke down and wept, overwhelmed with love for the young man who was like his own son.

'I have never heard of a man who spared his enemy,' he said at last.

'You are not my enemy,' David said.

The king turned away and left the place, but he still could not rid himself of his hatred and fear of David.

'This is the man who will take your kingdom away from you,' his voices reminded him.

Still Saul hunted David, and still David fled from Saul. Once again David had the chance to kill him, when he found him sleeping in a field. The king had brought an army of soldiers to slay David and his gang of outlaws. But David had no hatred for Saul.

He took the king's spear, but he spared his life. Then he stood on a hill and shouted to waken the king's army.

'Will no one guard the king?' he shouted. 'You have left him sleeping, without even a spear at his side!'

King Saul woke up and recognized David's voice. 'Is that my son, David? Is that my beloved son?'

Again he knew that David had had the chance to kill him, and had spared his life. But there was no reconciliation. David knew that the king was an ill man, that his emotions were out of control, and that nothing would shake away his desire to get rid of David. It was in his blood now, it was the force that drove him from day to day, and nothing would stop him until the deed was done.

'Seek him by sunlight, seek him by moonlight, seek him by starlight, but kill him,' the voices urged. 'Samuel the prophet told you that a man would take your kingdom away. Will you let him, Saul?'

'No,' Saul moaned. 'David must die.'

There was only one thing that David could do. He must leave the land of the Israelites. He would never be safe there. He would never have a home again. With a heavy heart he crossed the border into the land of his people's greatest enemy: the Philistines.

My God, oh my God,
Why have you forsaken me?
Why are you so far away
That you cannot hear me?
Oh my God, by night and day
I cry to you in vain
And I can never rest.

FROM PSALM 22

David the King

The great prophet Samuel was an old man by now, and when he died, the whole of Israel mourned him. King Saul was wretched with despair. Even though he was afraid of Samuel because of the prophecy he had made, he missed the holy man.

And he missed David, though he himself had hounded him out of the country. David was now living with his greatest enemy, fighting with them. He had become a Philistine, and he was lost to Saul for ever.

'Will I never see him again?' the king grieved. 'I called him my son, and I have lost him. And will I never be able to unburden my soul to God, now Samuel has left this earth? I am alone.'

Jonathan tried to console him. He was loyal and loving to his father through all the years of his madness even though he missed David, too, and wanted him back. David had been his greatest friend, and they had loved one another like brothers. And Israel, too, mourned the loss of David the warrior. Israel had become great when David was in command of its armies. Now the borders were shrinking again; invading armies ransacked the towns and villages. And at last news came that the Philistines were massing their armies to invade Israel again. In the past they had taken half of Israel's land. Now they were preparing to take it all. Hundreds and thousands of soldiers were gathered at the foot of Mount Gilboa, and more were coming, and more.

King Saul prayed for help, but God had deserted him and no answer came. None of his advisers could tell him what to do.

'If no one alive will help me, I must seek counsel from the dead,' he decided. Long ago he had banished witches and mediums from his country, people who were in touch with the dead and could speak to their shades. Now he asked if any of these women were still practising, and he was told, yes, there was a woman at Endor.

'Then I will see her,' he decided. 'I will try to raise the ghost of Samuel.'

He went in disguise to the witch's cave, knowing that she would be afraid if she knew who he was. He covered his face with his cloak so she wouldn't recognize him and asked her if she could help him to speak to the dead prophet. She answered cautiously, her voice no more than a whisper, glancing around her all the time to make sure no one was around.

'It is very dangerous these days,' she croaked. 'If the king knew, we would both be killed.'

'I know that,' Saul said. 'Get on with it.'

She led him into the dark cave, where a small fire crackled on a bed of twigs. She threw a handful of crystals onto the flames and instantly the smoke became thick and black, and then burned green, red, and gold.

She gasped and held out her hands, seeing something that made her cower with fear.

'What do you see?' Saul asked.

'I see an old man with a grey beard,' she moaned. 'He is going to speak.' She closed her eyes, and out of her mouth came the words of the prophet Samuel.

'Why have you roused me from my death? Oh, why will you not let me sleep?'

King Saul went down on his knees. 'The Philistines are invading my kingdom,' he whispered. 'Holy Samuel, tell me what I can do?'

'You were warned, and you would not listen. Listen now; this is what will happen. David will become king. The Philistines will conquer Israel, and you and your sons will die.'

'When? When will this be?'

'Tomorrow.'

Meanwhile, more and more Philistine soldiers were marching towards Mount Gilboa, and among them was David. When they recognized who he was, the other Philistine soldiers refused to march with him.

'He's a Hebrew, he shouldn't be marching to fight his own people,' they said. 'He's led armies against us, time and time again. How can we trust him to fight with us?'

So the captain sent David away and told him to wait until he had news that the battle was over. It was a long, anxious time for David. Three days later, a messenger came running to him and David went out to meet him, eager and worried.

'What news?' he called.

'We are victorious,' the messenger said. 'The king's army has fallen.'

David's heart sank. 'What news of King Saul and Jonathan?'

'Dead, both of them.' And the messenger handed him Saul's crown.

David went down on his knees, the crown clasped tight in his fists, overwhelmed with grief. He went straight to the scene of the battle and searched among the bodies there, and found that it was true. Jonathan had been killed on the battlefield. But he could not find Saul.

'Where is my king?' he asked, and one of the Israelite soldiers told him what had happened.

'We've taken his body away. King Saul met his fate bravely. He was wounded, and rather than give himself up to the Philistines, he killed himself with his own sword.'

'Saul and Jonathan, my father, my brother,' David wept.

'Beloved and lovely, to me and to each other.

In life and in death they were close to one another.

They were swifter than eagles, and stronger than lions.

How the mighty have fallen.'

That was one of David's finest songs, and has never been forgotten.

> *Save me*
> *For the waters have come up to my neck*
> *I am sinking in deep mud*
> *There is nothing for me to stand on*
> *I have come into deep waters*
> *And the tide sweeps over me . . .*

FROM PSALM 69

The City of David

So David returned and was anointed King of Judah at Hebron. The first thing he did was to reward those Israelites who had carried Saul's body away from the battlefield and buried him with all the respect due to a great king. Then he vowed to reclaim the land that the Philistines had taken, and that became his life's mission, to rebuild the country that was his true home. Finally, after seven years, he was anointed king of Israel and Judah. He decided that the city of Jerusalem was to be his home. But the trouble was, it didn't belong to him, it belonged to the Jebusites. They refused to let him come anywhere near it.

'You can't have our city!' they shouted from the walls. 'We'll never open our gates to let you in. Every man of us will fight to keep you away, even the blind men, even the crippled men; you'll never take our city away from us.'

'I hate them as much as they hate me,' David said. 'They won't stop me.'

He set up camp outside the walls with his followers, and thought of a brilliant plan that would help him to get into Jerusalem. He sent two of his men to scramble up the water shafts that led under the walls and into the heart of the city. In no time the men emerged and ran to open the gates, and the Israelites poured through in their thousands, shouting and cheering: 'This is the City of David.'

The Jebusites could do nothing to stop them.

But the Israelites were still not contented. It was a fine new home, a beautiful city, but the heart of their community was missing. They sent their elders to speak to David. 'Listen, you are our flesh and blood,' they told him. 'We are one family. You are the shepherd who has led us to your holy city. But where is the Ark of the Covenant? It should be with us wherever we go.'

David agreed with them, and the Ark was sent for. Four priests in white robes were appointed to carry it through the gates of the city. The Ark was lifted on its long poles and rested on a cart, because no one was allowed to touch it, ever. But as the cart was being trundled up the muddy track that led up the hill to Jerusalem one of the wheels got stuck in the mud, the cart swayed sideways, and the Ark began to slide. Without thinking twice, one of the priests, whose name was Uzzah, put out his hand to steady it, and the second his hand touched the Ark he was struck dead.

David was afraid when he saw this. 'I'm not ready yet for the Ark to be brought in,' he said. 'How can I take responsibility for it when such a terrible thing has happened? Leave it outside the gates until I decide what to do.'

He arranged for the Ark to be left with a family, and it rested in their house for three months. It was a wonderful honour for them. During that time the people of the household were blessed with happiness and good fortune.

Still the Israelites begged David to bring the Ark into the city. 'It belongs here,' they told him. 'It goes everywhere with us. If we make Jerusalem our home, then the Ark must be here too.'

So David consented, and at last the Ark was brought into Jerusalem. The priests and the people followed it in a noisy procession; everybody danced round it, shouting and singing, shaking tambourines, banging

drums and playing pipes and trumpets, and David himself threw off his royal robes and danced with the people in the streets.

His wife, Michal, was watching from their house; alone of the Israelites, she refused to join in the celebrating. Even after the Ark was placed in a ceremonial tent of gorgeous billowing fabrics, gold and red and midnight blue, she refused to come outside to see it. Even when the feasting and drinking started, she kept inside, watching from the window, with her lips curled in displeasure and disapproval.

'Why didn't you join in the celebrating?' David asked her that night, when at last the singers and dancers slept and the lamps were blown out.

'Shame on you!' Michal hissed. 'You call yourself a king, and yet you dance in the streets half-naked, like a common labourer. I was ashamed to see such vulgar behaviour.'

'Nothing I do is shameful,' David answered. 'I do it for the glory of God. Why should a king be ashamed to dance and sing and eat with his people? You are the shameful one, for criticizing me.'

It happened that from that day Michal's womb closed, and she was never able to have children. David took many women to his bed, whenever he pleased. He had many children, but not one of them was Michal's.

He lived in a beautiful house made of sweet-scented cedar, a house that was truly fit for a king, in the golden city that would always be

named after him; yet things were still not right, and perhaps David did have reason to be ashamed. One day Nathan the prophet came to tell him that God wanted to speak to him.

'Tell me,' David said. 'What does God want to say?'

When he heard the voice of God coming through Nathan's mouth David sank to his knees and bowed his head. He closed his eyes and looked inside himself, and saw again the little shepherd boy who had sung and played his pipe in the long ago and far-away hills of his childhood.

David, remember the fields around your father's home.
Remember the day I entered your heart?
I have never left you, David.
I left Saul,
I let him plunge into darkness,
but I have never left you,
and I never will.
I have been with my people
wherever they have gone.
Now you have found a home.
From your home the son of man will come,
from your children, David,
will come the one who will save my people.

David breathed slowly. Surely he had been blessed enough, to rise from shepherd to king. Could it really be true that the saviour of Israel would be one of his own flesh and blood? He was not yet ready for such greatness. And then he knew what God was asking of him.

A home. This is my home, David.

Yet the place in which God himself had his earthly home, where the Ark of the Covenant was kept, was a tent! How could this be, when David had the finest house that any man in the city could have lived in?

'I will make you a home,' he promised. 'That is my task, Lord.'

But it was not David who built a temple for the Ark. War put an end to that promise. War, and love.

The lord is my shepherd.
I have everything.
When I am tired, he lets me sleep
in green meadows.
And by day he leads me to still water
where I can drink my fill.
He makes me whole again,
my body and my soul.

FROM PSALM 23

Bathsheba

The woman's name was Bathsheba, and it has to be said that she was very beautiful. King David watched her bathing and fell passionately in love with her.

'Who is that woman?' he asked. 'Find out, because I want her.'

'Excuse me; I know who she is,' one of his advisers said. 'But she is already married.'

'Tssh!' said David angrily. 'That wasn't my question. Who is she?'

'Her name is Bathsheba,' the adviser said. 'And she is married—'

'Tssh! You've already told me that.'

'To a general in your army, King David. His name is Uriah the Hittite.'

'If he's a general in my army, then he's well occupied at the moment,' David said. 'Send her to me.'

So Bathsheba was sent for, and King David treated her as if she were his own wife, while Michal sighed in her lonely room and Uriah the Hittite risked his life to save Jerusalem from invaders. It wasn't long before Bathsheba told David that she was expecting his child. David sent at once for Uriah and told him to go to his wife, but the general refused.

'It's not a time for me to hide safe and sound with my wife,' he said. 'There's a war on, and my place is on the battlefield.' He might have thought that King David's place was on the battlefield too, but he didn't dare say it. 'The Ark is still in a tent, the country is at war. Soldiers are sleeping on the battlefield, not in their beds.'

David was very angry. He sent Uriah back to the battlefield with a letter for Joab, the commander of the army. The letter read, 'Put Uriah in the front line where the fighting is fiercest. When the others draw back, leave him out there.'

'So,' said Joab, folding away the letter. 'You've displeased the king.'

'I've done nothing,' said Uriah. 'My only wish is to serve in his army.'

As David hoped, Uriah was killed on the battlefield. Bathsheba was given a little time to mourn for him, then she brought her child to the cedar house and lived with David as his wife. But God was not pleased with him, and sent Nathan the prophet to tell David so. This time Nathan spoke in his own voice, and he chose to tell David a story. Maybe it was because David was a poet that he chose to speak to him in this way. Maybe he felt that only the language of storytelling could touch David's heart. This was the story that he told:

'Once upon a time, in a land not far from here, there lived two men: a poor man and a rich man. The rich man had many fine flocks of sheep, and the poor man had one lamb. He loved that lamb as much as he would have loved a child. She ate from his dish, she slept in his arms. Now, one day, a weary traveller knocked at the rich man's door. He was thirsty and hungry and he begged for some supper to set him on his way. Of course, the rich man said, come in, come in. And do you know what he did? Do you think he sent for one of his fattest lambs to be butchered? No. He didn't do that. He stole the poor man's lamb, he killed it and cooked it and served it up for a meal. What do you think of that, David?'

'That's terrible,' David said. 'The rich man should be punished.'

'Well, you've behaved just as badly as that rich man,' Nathan said. 'Think. God has given you everything you wanted, and yet you have taken more. You will be punished, David. Your child will die.'

There was no stopping this punishment. Very soon Bathsheba's child became ill, and nothing, not prayer or medicine, love or grief, could save him.

David pleaded with God. He wouldn't eat or drink. He lay on the ground unable to move for sorrow. But it was no use. Within seven days the little boy was dead.

David and Absolom

King David had many sons, and his favourite was called Absolom. He was a very beautiful boy, with long flowing hair. David loved this son more than he loved his life. One day Absolom had a quarrel with one of his brothers and killed him in a fight. The news nearly broke David's heart.

'You have done a terrible thing,' David told him. 'You have killed your own brother, and you have nearly killed your father with grief.'

By law, Absolom should have been put to death, but David couldn't let that happen. So he thought of another punishment, one that spared Absolom's life, but which was very painful to David.

'You must be punished. But I will spare your life because I love you. This is your punishment: leave Jerusalem, Absolom. Go. You must never return to this city while I live.'

Absolom plotted to take revenge on his father for this punishment. He set up camp just outside the city gates and began to recruit an army of rebels who were willing to help him to overthrow the king. Then he sent a challenge to his father, to come out of the city and fight his rebel army.

The last thing King David wanted to do was to fight his own son. So he decided that, although the battle must take place, in the name of honour, he himself would not take part in it. He would leave the city so he couldn't even witness what was happening, and he would let his soldiers and Absolom's soldiers fight it out. He had no doubt that the scratch army that his son had pulled together would be defeated.

Before he went, he gave his captain, Joab, special orders.

'Be gentle with Absolom,' he said. 'Remember he is my son, and I love him.'

King David's army was victorious. The rebel army retreated, and Absolom fled to save his life. But as he rode through the woods, his long hair was caught in an overhanging branch of an oak tree. He struggled to get free but his mule rode on, leaving him dangling helplessly there. The more he twisted and turned to free himself, the tighter the knots of hair tangled in the branches.

The king's soldiers saw him hanging and left him, afraid to touch him.

'Absolom is caught in a tree,' they told Joab. 'We didn't know what to do so we've left him there.'

'Leave him to me,' Joab said.

He rode through the woods, following Absolom's cries of pain. When he reached him he reined in his horse and just stood watching.

'Help me!' Absolom shouted.

Joab drew out his sword, but instead of cutting Absolom's hair to release him, he drove his sword straight through the boy's heart.

'You may be the king's son, but you are his enemy,' the captain said, and watched the boy die.

When evening came, David returned to Jerusalem and sat by the gates of the city, anxiously waiting for news. A servant came slowly towards him, a dark figure against the burnished red of the sky. David rose to his feet.

'It's over. The rebels are defeated,' the servant said.

But something in his voice made David go cold. 'What other news?' he said. 'What news of my son?'

The servant turned his face away. 'Your son is dead.'

'Absolom? Not Absolom?' It was more than David could bear. He had lost his brother-friend, Jonathan. He had lost his father-king, Saul. And now he had lost his favourite son.

The sound of his music that day was the most haunting, lonely sound that man would ever hear. King David's song was a song of grief, and was heard all over the land, and is still heard to this day in the terrible aching grief of any man who has lost his child:

'Oh, my son Absolom, my son, my son Absolom.

If only I had died instead of you.

Oh, Absolom, my son, my son,

Oh, Absolom, my son.'

Solomon the Wise King

King David was growing old. He had many sons, and out of them all he chose one of the youngest, Solomon, to be the next king. This made Solomon's older brother, Adonijah, angry and jealous. He believed he had the right to the crown. He decided not to wait until David was dead, but had himself crowned by his supporters.

When David heard about this he shrugged his shoulders and said, 'What Adonijah does is his business, but he has no right to call himself king. I have chosen Solomon.'

He had the boy Solomon crowned officially, in front of his subjects. It was a day of public celebration, with bands playing, and people dancing and juggling and singing in the streets; the whole city rang with cheers as Solomon was paraded in front of everyone in his royal robes and crown. He looked as scared as he felt.

Adonijah was dining with his followers in another part of town that day, and when he heard the cheering and trumpet blowing and singing he sent one of the men to find out what was going on.

'Well,' said the man when he came back. 'Guess what? Your brother has been crowned King of all Israel.'

He didn't bow to Adonijah, but gave him the bad news and left as quickly as he could to join in the fun outside.

'But I'm the king!' Adonijah shouted. 'Everybody knows that!'

He turned to his men, but one by one they slipped away from the feast and went to join the party in the streets.

'Long live the king!' they shouted, along with all the crowds. 'Long live King Solomon!'

Adonijah was deeply afraid. He knew what he would do if he were in Solomon's place. He would kill him. So he ran to the altar for sanctuary and hid there, weeping and trembling and praying for mercy. When Solomon saw what a coward his brother had become he knew he was no longer his enemy, so he sent him back home.

But in his heart of hearts Solomon was still anxious about being king. It was a great gift from his father, but it was a great burden too. David was dead now. Solomon felt he was too young for such a burden of responsibility. He didn't know whether he was strong enough to carry it. And there was so much to learn. He decided to ask God for help.

He filled the altar of Gibeon with a thousand offerings, and lit great golden bowls of incense. The sweet perfume rose in spirals of smoke to heaven. Solomon fell asleep, and dreamed that God was gazing down at him. But the dream was more real than life itself. All the air was filled with sound, and he knew it was the voice of God.

Solomon. What do you want most?

Solomon could have asked for anything at all. He knew that, and he knew that God would grant any wish he made.

'Father, I am just like a little child,' he said. 'How can I be a good king, when I don't know anything? I have more subjects in my power than there are stars in the sky. They are your people. They are great people.'

Go on, Solomon. What do you want?

'I want to rule them as they deserve to be ruled. I want to be wise enough to know the difference between right and wrong. That's all I want.'

Now he had spoken the thoughts that were in his heart, and he waited in fear to know what God might say to him. Would God tell him he was not fit to be king, because he didn't know the difference between right and wrong?

The voice of God came back to him like a song:
Solomon, you could have asked for a long and happy life.
You could have asked for your enemies to be laid low.
You could have asked for wealth beyond your dreams.
But you asked to be wise, King Solomon.
And your wish will be granted.
You will be wiser than any king has ever been
You will be wiser than any king will ever be.

'Thank you, thank you, God,' said Solomon, on his knees with gratitude. 'You have given me the only thing I want.'

But when he stood up again to leave the altar of Gibeon, God spoke to him again.

Wait, Solomon. I will also give you things you did not ask for.

Solomon sank to his knees again.

Riches, glory, honour, and a long life.
You shall have all these things, because they are fitting
for a king who is so wise.

Solomon woke up then and rubbed his eyes. He gazed round him, with the words still lingering like music in his head. He knew it had all been a dream, but he also knew that it would all come true. He would have the wisdom that he had asked for, to help him to be a good king.

He said many things that made people think about themselves and why they did things, such as:

Like vinegar is acid to the teeth,
Like smoke makes our eyes sting,
So lazy workers are to their employers.

Like a gold ring in a pig's snout
Is a beautiful woman who has no sense.

Go to the ant, you lazybones.
Consider its ways and be wise.

And it wasn't long before the power of his wisdom was put to the test.

Two women came to his court for help. They had a problem that no one had been able to solve for them. They were carrying a wicker basket, each one holding a handle, and when they put it down, Solomon could see that there was a baby boy inside.

'Whose is this baby?' he asked.

'Mine,' they both said.

Solomon folded his arms and waited for them to tell him their story.

'We live in the same house,' one of the women said.

'And we both had baby sons at the same time.'

'Then you should be friends,' Solomon said.

'We were,' they both said.

He nodded, and waited for them to speak again.

'Something terrible happened,' the first woman said. 'She killed her baby. She didn't mean to. She rolled on top of him in her sleep and when she woke up, the poor child was dead.'

'That is indeed a terrible thing to happen,' said King Solomon.

'But it's not true!' the second woman said. She started crying. 'How could I kill my child? *She* killed *her* baby in her sleep. And then she stole mine.'

'I didn't, I didn't,' the first woman sobbed. 'She stole my son and put her dead baby in his place.'

'No I didn't,' the second woman screamed. 'She stole my son and pretended he was hers.'

'He's mine,' the first woman said, lifting the baby out of the cradle. 'Look, he has my eyes.'

The second woman snatched him from her. 'He's mine. Your baby is dead. Your baby is dead.'

'Stop!' King Solomon said, but there was no stopping them now. The baby was snatched from one to the other, and they were all crying now, mother and kidnapper and baby, kidnapper, mother and baby, all three of them, filling the court with their anger and grief. The two women squabbled and cried and begged King Solomon to choose between them, who was the real mother, who should keep the child.

'There is only one way to solve this,' King Solomon said at last. 'Bring me a sword.'

A silence like winter fell over the court. A servant ran to the armoury and came back bearing the king's own sword, and handed it to Solomon.

'This is my solution,' the king said. 'I am going to cut this baby in half. You will each have a half, and then you will be satisfied.'

He put the baby on a table in front of him, and raised the sword above his head, clutching the handle with both hands.

'No!' the first woman screamed. 'No, please spare the baby's life. Give him to her, she can have him. But please spare this little baby's life.'

'Cut him in half,' the second woman said. 'She'll never be satisfied. Cut him in half, and we'll share him.'

King Solomon lowered the sword. He lifted up the baby and placed him in the first woman's arms. 'You are the real mother,' he said. 'Take him, and go in peace, both of you.'

That was the first judgement that King Solomon made, and he is famous for it, from the north to the south of the world, and from the east to the west of the world, and from that day to this.

King Solomon's Temple

Because of the constant threat of war, King David had never been able to build the temple that he had promised God, but now in Solomon's reign there was peace and harmony, and the time was right. Solomon wrote to King Hiram of Tyre, who had been his father's friend, and suggested that their servants work together to build the temple. He would give them all whatever wage they were used to.

'It must be made only of the beautiful cedar of Lebanon,' he wrote. 'Nothing else looks so fine or smells so sweet; nothing else is so strong. And nobody but the Sidonians know how to cut the timber properly.'

Hiram agreed to have the trees felled and transported down-river by rafts. Thirty thousand Israelites went to the Lebanon in shifts of ten thousand every month—a month of work, two months of rest for every man. And in the meantime, eighty thousand labourers stayed at home to cut and prepare the stone for the temple's foundations.

Imagine the sweat and the toil of the labourers in the dusty, yellow heat; imagine the heaving of stone from the massive quarries, and the crash of thousands of felled trees. Day after day the men laboured, week after week and month after month for seven years. Imagine the height and the width of the greatest temple that had ever been built. Imagine two carved cherubs that were so huge that their wings spread across an entire wall. There were carvings of palm trees and flowers and angels, every surface was made beautiful. And then the whole thing was coated in pure gold. Imagine how it gleamed.

At last it was ready. In the seventh month of the seventh year all the priests gathered together, and the heads and elders of all the twelve tribes of the twelve sons of Jacob, and they fetched the Ark of the Covenant from the holy tent where it had rested for so many, many years. Every sheep and cow and goat that could be gathered on that day was slaughtered and sacrificed. Imagine the bleating and lowing, the terror and the silence. And then the Ark was carried to the temple and placed in the inner room with the huge carved cherubs.

What was in the Ark of the Covenant? This: two stones. And what were the stones? Remember Moses? Remember Mount Sinai, blazing red in the light of the setting sun, and how Moses climbed to the summit with the voice of God in his head? Remember the Ten Commandments?

And imagine this: a cloud of smoke billows through Solomon's temple the day the Ark is placed there. The smoke is so thick that one man cannot see another, so silent that it seems as if the world has lost its breath, so holy that every man of Israel knows that it is the spirit of God, filling at last the house that Solomon has built for him.

Rehoboam the Foolish King

Solomon's son Rehoboam became the next king, after his father's death. When Solomon's official, Jeraboam, heard about this he returned from his exile in Egypt, where he had fled from Solomon.

'Make life easier for us than your father did,' he said to Rehoboam. 'King Solomon put such a heavy burden round our necks that we were like the beasts of the field, the yoked oxen pulling the plough. You can be a better king than he was. Lighten our load, and we'll serve you gladly.'

Rehoboam told him he wanted to think about this. Should he rule like his father, or should he become a different sort of king?

'Go away for three days,' he told Jeraboam. 'When you come back, I'll have decided what sort of king I want to be. I'll take advice.'

Well, that was a wise thing to do, and his father would have been pleased with that. But Rehoboam took the wrong advice, and divided Israel for ever.

The older men who had served King Solomon gave him one sort of advice; the younger men of his own generation gave him another. These were the choices: the older men told him to be lenient, to be a servant of his own people, so they would love him and want to serve him. And the young men said just the opposite. 'Your father was harsh, you must be harsher. The people staggered under his burden; make them go down on their knees. They will respect you and serve you if you do this.'

On the third day, Jeraboam and his followers came to Rehoboam for an answer.

'What kind of king will you be?' they asked him.

He held out his hand towards them and splayed out his fingers. 'I have more strength in my little finger than my father had in his entire body,' he told them. 'You will bow down to me with the weight of the load I will put upon your shoulders. My father scourged you with whips; I will lash you with scorpions.'

'Then the house of David is lost to us,' the people of Jeraboam said. 'We cannot live here. We will take to our tents and live as nomads, we will wander the desert, we will hide in the mountains, but we cannot live here with you.'

Just as he had promised, Rehoboam was a tyrant over the Israelites who remained in Judah. His taskmaster beat them and forced them to build and farm and toil for him, and one day they rebelled and stoned the taskmaster to death. When he knew they had turned against him, Rehoboam fled to Jerusalem, and ruled there. Meanwhile the Israelites made Jeraboam king, and under him they worshipped the false gods. So the land of Israel was divided and there were now two kings—Rehoboam, king of Judah, in the south and Jeraboam, king of Israel, in the north. Rehoboam raised an army to try to gain back his kingdom, but the voice of God spoke to him through one of his holy men:

You shall not fight against the people of Israel. Send everyone home.

It was too late. Israel was lost.

Elijah the Prophet

Israel had many bad kings, but the worst of all was Ahab. He made God angrier than any other king had ever done. Perhaps the worst thing Ahab did was to marry Jezebel.

Jezebel worshipped the false god of Baal, and she insisted that everyone in Israel must worship it too. She made Ahab send his soldiers into all the towns and cities to make sure that her god was being worshipped, and gave them orders to kill anyone who disobeyed her. Everyone was afraid.

Only one man stood against Jezebel and her false god. His name was Elijah, and he was a prophet. He watched what was happening to the people of Israel; he saw how they were losing their God, and he knew that he, and only he, could save them.

One day when Jezebel and Ahab were feasting Elijah strode in and faced them.

'What are you doing here?' Jezebel demanded.

'I've come to speak to Ahab,' Elijah answered. He was so angry at the way Jezebel made Ahab treat his own people that he wasn't afraid. 'I've come to tell him how his wickedness will be repaid.' And he turned to the king and said, 'Because of your sins, there will be a drought upon Israel; no rain will fall, no dew will form; the rivers will cease to run. And after the drought there will be three years of famine.'

'Kill this man,' Jezebel said to her husband.

Go, said God. *Go, Elijah, man of God. I will protect you.*

Elijah left the palace at once.
Jezebel's soldiers searched for him, but
he was nowhere to be found, because
God's angel led him to a safe place, far away in the wilderness.
Elijah found a stream to drink from, and every morning and
every night ravens came with bread and meat for him. Yet he was
lonely. He felt he was the only man of God left in Israel. He knew
that God was a jealous God, who punished men for their
disobedience and for the sins of their fathers. God would destroy
Israel because of the sins of Ahab and Jezebel. The children of Israel
were dying, parched with thirst, and there was no comfort or help for
the people till they turned back to him. But this had happened before,
when the Israelites fled from Egypt.

'If they turn to God, he will be merciful, and they will survive,' he told
himself, and he prayed that this would happen.

Day after day the sun burned in a yellow sky. No soft rain fell to relieve
the dry air; the nights were as hot as the days, and no dew formed. Soon
even the stream that Elijah had been drinking from dried up. Like all the
people of Israel, he would die of thirst if God didn't help him.

Elijah, go to Zarephath.

A widow woman will sustain you;

her oil and oatmeal will never fail

until the rains wash the earth again.

As Elijah journeyed towards the coast, he saw how
the drought had parched the fields. Nothing
grew. The cattle sank to their knees and died;
the peasants and farmers were skin and bone,
their children sobbed for water and food.
There was nothing he could do to help
them; he, too, was dying of hunger.

Just outside the city gates at Zarephath he saw a widow woman on her hands and knees scratching round for bits of twigs, and he knew this was the woman his angel had sent him to find.

'Give me food and water,' he begged her. 'I am a man of God.'

She lifted her hands in despair. 'I've nothing to give you,' she said. 'With this handful of sticks I will be lighting a fire to cook the few grains of oatmeal I have left, the few drops of oil. It will be our last meal. After this, my young son and I will close our eyes and die.'

'Go home,' Elijah told her. 'Make me a cake with your oil and your oatmeal, and after that your pots will never be empty.'

She was too weak with hunger to argue. Her son was sick and would surely die anyway. So the woman did as she was told and used up the last of her oil and oatmeal and gave the cake to Elijah. Her son lay in his bed and watched her and said nothing.

When Elijah had eaten, he gestured to the woman to look in the oatmeal barrel and the oil jar.

'Full to the brim!' she gasped. 'How could this happen?'

'I am a man of God,' Elijah reminded her. 'And he is merciful to me.'

'Now I believe you,' she said. 'And I believe in your God.'

Elijah made his home with the woman and the boy, and lived in the loft of their house, and they never fell short of food again. But one day the boy fell desperately ill. Within hours he was lying motionless on his bed. The widow screamed for Elijah to come.

'You've brought this on us, you and your jealous God!' she sobbed. 'Have you come here to remind me of my sins and to kill my son? There's no breath left in him. He's dead. My son is dead. Why? Why have you done this to us?'

Elijah took the child in his arms, and gazed down at him, with sorrow heavy in his heart. It was true, there was no breath left in him. He carried the boy up the ladder to his room in the loft and laid him down on his own bed.

'God, why have you done this?' he asked. 'Why have you brought sorrow and grief to this good woman, when she gave me her last oil and oatmeal? How could you take her son away from her like this? You are a God of mercy and compassion. Give the boy his soul again. Let him live.'

Elijah stretched himself over the child and breathed into his mouth, three times, and on the third time the boy opened his eyes and stared at him in wonder.

'Come quickly!' Elijah shouted. 'Your son is alive!'

The widow scrambled up the ladder and cradled her child in her arms as she had cradled him on the day he was born. 'He was dead, and now he lives!' she wept and laughed at the same time, beside herself with relief and amazement and joy. 'Now I believe you are a man of God, Elijah! And I believe in your God.'

Three years passed, and still the famine parched the land. Israel was faint with hunger. The earth was dying, the people were dying, and still Jezebel made them worship her god of Baal.

'Is there no end to this suffering?' Elijah asked in his heart. 'Is there nothing I can do to turn the people away from the false gods?'

The time is now come for you to go to Ahab.

I will bless the earth with rain.

Elijah journeyed back away from the coast and into the heart of the country, and saw again the destruction that three years of drought and famine had brought about.

'Is there no end to it?' people wailed, and their tired voices echoed over the silent fields and empty streets.

'Only one person can end it,' Elijah told them, and made his way to Ahab's palace.

The king ordered his soldiers to surround the prophet and bring him to the inner court at once. The guards jostled him roughly but Elijah walked with them, silent and dignified, and stood facing the king and queen, totally unafraid.

'So you have come back, Elijah!' King Ahab roared. 'You have done this! You have brought my people to their knees.'

'Oh no, Ahab,' Elijah said quietly. '*You* have brought *God's* people to their knees. You and your fathers have sinned against him. You have forsaken God. If you had not worshipped Jezebel's god, none of this would have happened.'

'Kill him!' Jezebel ordered, but Elijah was not afraid of her, and didn't even look at her.

'Listen to me, Ahab. If you want the rains to fall on the earth of Israel, you must ask God to help you. Bring all the people of Israel to Mount Carmel, and all the prophets of Baal, and all Jezebel's followers. Make two sacrifices, one to your god, one to mine, and we will see whose god is the true God.'

'This will be an easy contest,' Jezebel laughed. 'You are a fool, Elijah, but we'll play this game before we kill you, to make sure all our people see Elijah the prophet on his knees with shame.'

All Israel was summoned, and those who were well enough flocked to Mount Carmel. They came because Jezebel ordered them to, and they were afraid of her; and they came because by now there wasn't a soul who had not heard of Elijah the prophet who had foretold three years of famine, and who now foretold rain. He was famous, and they wanted to see him before Jezebel had him put to death.

'We will build two altars of stone, and build a trench around them, and put wood across them,' Elijah ordered. 'We must put a bullock on each, for the sacrifice. But we must not set fire to either of them.'

Mystified, the priests of Baal did as they were told, and placed a bullock on their altar. Elijah did the same.

'Who will light the fires?' Jezebel sneered.

'God will. You call on your god, and I'll call on mine, the God of Abraham and Isaac, the God of Israel. Whichever god answers is the true God.'

There was a murmur of excitement among the priests and people gathered there. They watched Jezebel and Elijah.

'You accept the challenge?'

'Of course,' said Jezebel.

'Call on your god first, and then I will call on the Lord of Israel,' Elijah said.

Jezebel nodded to her prophets and they began to dance round the altar they had made, calling on Baal to answer them. Baal was silent.

'Is your god asleep? Is he away at the moment?' Elijah asked. 'He's very quiet. Call all your gods to help him. Call your mountain gods and forest gods, perhaps they'll hear you!'

The priests of Baal sang louder; they crashed their drums and blared their trumpets, they banged on tambourines, they skipped and jumped and slashed at themselves with knives, they worked themselves into a frenzy, but when they dropped to their knees with exhaustion there was no sign or sound from Baal, and their sacrifice was untouched.

'So,' said Elijah. 'I will call on my Lord.'

Then Elijah asked his followers to empty the last drops of precious water from their kidskin bottles over the other altar. One by one they came forward and shook out their skins until the bullock streamed with water. The wood was soaked through, and the water ran into the trench around the altar.

'Can I light a fire in all this water?' Elijah asked the people.

They shook their heads, mystified.

'No.' Jezebel smiled. 'It is impossible.'

'You are right,' said Elijah. 'I can't set fire to water. But God can.' He went onto his knees and stretched out his hands, and spoke quietly in his heart. 'Lord God of Abraham and Isaac and Israel, show these people that you are the true God. Let them know you and love you as I do. Hear me and answer me.'

Immediately a dazzling tongue of flame leapt down from heaven to earth. It licked up the bullock, it licked up the wood, it licked up the stone, the water in the trench, the earth around it. And all that remained was a scorch mark on the ground.

'Truly,' whispered the people of Israel, hushed with awe. 'This is the real God.'

'Truly,' said Elijah. 'This is the God of Abraham, of Isaac, of Israel.'

But Elijah had not finished yet. His anger against the priests of Baal was so great that he ordered his followers to take them all, all four hundred and fifty priests of Baal and slay them, every one. He showed no mercy.

Then he heard a sound that no others could hear, very faint, very far away. He sent his servant boy up to the top of the mountain. 'What can you see, child?' he called.

The boy looked over the sea. All he could see was the sky and the sea, as bright and hard as brass.

'Look again,' Elijah called. 'Look again.'

Seven times he called, and then at last the boy could see a tiny cloud like the fist of a man, and then the sky grew as grey as lead, and then as black as obsidian, and the rains came, gushing like the sea itself, drenching the parched earth, and quenched the terrible thirst of Israel.

Elijah in the Wilderness

'Kill him!' Jezebel screamed. 'He brought drought on the land. He brought famine, he brought death. And now he has killed my priests. Kill him! He has mocked my gods! Kill Elijah! Find him and kill him!'

Elijah fled for his life into the vast, empty wilderness. He was in despair now, knowing that Jezebel would force her false gods on to the people of Israel again, and that everything he had done would be for nothing. He walked in the emptiness until he was too weary to walk any further, and then he sank down under a juniper tree, and he had never known such hopelessness, such heaviness of heart. He begged God to allow him to die.

'I have finished, Lord. All I want is to bring your people back to you,' he said, 'but I am alone. I wanted Israel to listen to me. Why did you let them turn against you? There is no one to help me, and I am weary and afraid. They seek my life, they are spreading a net to catch me, and I have no strength against them. It is enough, God. Let me die.'

He lay down under the tree and closed his eyes, waiting for death.

But God was not ready to take him. Elijah drifted into a restless sleep, and felt a hand on his shoulder. He woke to find his angel standing over him, spreading wings like bright red flames across him. The warmth of hope spread over Elijah then, and the angel disappeared. Elijah sat up and found a cake of bread warm on a stone at his feet, and a crock of water at his side. He ate and drank, and fell into a peaceful sleep, and once again his angel touched his shoulder.

Wake up, Elijah. Eat and drink;
your journey is not yet over.
You must go to the holy mountain Horeb,
and there you will find a cave to rest in.
I will watch over you.
I will protect you and guide you.

Again there was water and warm bread for him. Elijah ate and drank again, and when he felt strong enough he set off on the long journey to Mount Horeb. It took him forty days and forty nights to reach it, and the food that the angel had given him sustained him during all this time. When he arrived at the mountain it was night. The fiery light of his angel led him to a cave, and he lay down and slept.

Elijah. Elijah. What are you doing here?

Elijah woke with a start. He knew at once that it was the voice of God himself that he could hear. He ran to the mouth of the cave, and there was his angel waiting for him. He followed his light to the top of the mountain. All around him a purple hurricane was blowing, so fierce that it split mountains apart, it flung boulders into the sky, but the angel wrapped his wings round Elijah and he was not harmed. After the hurricane came a green earthquake which made the ground below tremble and crack, but the angel protected him and Elijah was not harmed. Yet he still had not seen God. He waited on the mountain, and after the earthquake came a yellow eruption of fire and smoke, belching up to the sky like a great furnace, showering rocks and bubbling sulphur around him, but he sheltered inside the angel's wings with his cloak across his face, and waited.

Then came a silence that was so deep that it seemed as if the world itself had given up its ghost and died. The angel opened out his wings and Elijah listened to the terrible silence, and knew that mountains could be destroyed, that the whole world could shake with earthquakes, that great fires could come, and that God would still be there. And he knew that at that moment he was in the presence of God.

Elijah, Elijah. What are you doing here?

Elijah drew the cloak away from his face.

'I was afraid because I was alone. Israel turned away from you, and I had no one to help me to call the people back,' Elijah said, and waited to know whether God had heard him and would answer. And the answer came.

You are not alone, Elijah.
Anoint a new prophet.
His name is Elisha,
and he will take your place.
The new kings, Hazael and Jehu
will kill everyone who stood against me,
but seven thousand will be left.
These seven thousand
did not turn against me to worship Baal.
They will build a new Israel in my name.
Go in peace and do as I say.

The knowledge that he wasn't on his own any longer filled Elijah with eagerness and energy and the joy of being alive. He set off immediately for Damascus, and there in a field he saw a young man ploughing with twelve yoke of oxen, with a wake of birds following him.

'What is your name?' he called.

'Elisha,' the ploughman answered. Elijah smiled. He had found the man who would take his place and carry on his work, just as God had promised. He sat at the side of the field, peacefully watching until the young man had finished his work, and then he went over to him and took off his cloak and laid it over Elisha's shoulders.

'What does this mean?' Elisha asked, surprised. 'Am I to follow you?'

'A new time is coming,' Elijah said. 'Ahab and Jezebel will die. There will be a king of Syria called Hazael, and Jehu will be king of Israel. I will anoint them, and then you, Elisha, will be the prophet of the lord God of Abraham, Isaac, and Israel.'

'I don't understand,' said Elisha, shaking his head. 'But I'll gladly be your servant.'

From that time on, Elisha never left the old man's side. Together they went to Ahab and warned him that the kingdom of Syria would rise up against Israel, and that he would lose his life in the war. Ahab refused to believe him. He tried to cheat death by disguising himself as a common soldier, but death found him out on the battlefield. And Elijah knew then that it was his own time to die.

'Leave me now,' he said to Elisha. 'I need to be alone.'

But Elisha refused to leave his side. They travelled together to the ancient city of Jericho. It was night when they arrived, and Elijah went into a lodging house to sleep, but Elisha sat at the door, waiting and watching, unable to rest. In the deep darkness just before dawn he saw the flicker of torchlight on the walls and heard a group of white-robed men asking for him.

'I'm here,' he said.

'We are the prophets of Jericho,' one of the men said. 'Did you know that God is taking Elijah away from you today?'

'I know,' said Elisha. 'But I want to stay with him till the end.'

Dawn came swiftly, but before the rest of the town stirred, Elijah left his room in the lodging house and came outside to Elisha.

'I am going on now,' he said. 'You stay here.'

'As long as you live, I will live with you,' Elisha said.

They walked in silence together to the river Jordan, and the prophets of Jericho followed them. When they came to the banks of the river the other prophets drew away, wondering what would happen, but Elijah and Elisha went right to the water's edge.

'I must cross to the other side,' said Elijah.

'And I will go with you,' Elisha said. 'I want to stay with you for all time.'

Elijah took off his cloak and struck the water with it, and the river rolled apart so a path of dry land spread from one bank to the other. Elijah and Elisha crossed together, and when they reached the other side the waters closed behind them again.

'Now is the time,' Elijah said. 'My journey is over.' He turned to Elisha and knew the young man's sorrow. 'What can I give you, Elisha?'

'Give me your spirit,' Elisha said, and Elijah embraced him as if he were his own son.

'That is a hard thing to ask for,' he said. 'I don't know if that is possible.'

They heard the whinnying of horses, and looked up to see a chariot of fire descending from the sky, drawn by four golden stallions, with flames whirling from their nostrils and sparks like comets showering from their tails and manes and hooves. Elijah and Elisha released each other and the chariot came to rest between them. Elijah climbed into the chariot, and a whirlwind of fire rushed round him and drew him up, up high towards heaven. He took off his cloak and tossed it down.

'Father, oh father, oh my father Elijah!' Elisha wept. He tore his clothes and fell on his knees in grief, and then he saw Elijah's cloak lying on the ground. He picked it up and held it close. It was still warm; it still had the earthly smell of his master. He went back to the banks of the river and beat the water with the cloak as Elijah had done, and the river rolled into two halves. A dry path opened up, and he took one last sorrowing look at the spot where he and Elijah had stood embracing, and crossed over to the other side.

There were the prophets of Jericho, waiting for him, and when they saw how the river opened up for him and closed behind him they went down on their knees to him.

'You are the new prophet of Israel.'

Elisha draped the cloak around his shoulders. 'The spirit of Elijah is with me,' he said. 'And always will be, until my task on earth is done.'

Elisha and the Leper

Israel was always at war with one or another of its neighbours. Sometimes the Israelites won, sometimes they didn't, but the wars and raids never stopped. They lost people and land, they lost wealth, and sometimes they lost their children because invaders stole them to be slaves.

Namaan, the captain of the Syrian army, took a little Israelite girl home after one of the raids, and gave her to his wife. The little girl longed for home, and talked about Israel all the time. She remembered the stories her mother had told her when they were gathering figs or pressing oil together. Her mistress liked to hear them because they took her mind off a terrible illness that had suddenly struck her husband. Namaan had leprosy. His skin was covered in silvery white flakes of dead flesh, and there was no feeling in his hands. Every day she and the little girl prepared healing oils for his skin, but he never got better. He was irritable and impatient with them both. Everybody else avoided him because they were terrified of catching leprosy from him, and he wrapped his robes round himself so no one would see how disfigured he was.

'Tell me your stories,' his wife would say to the little girl. 'See if you can cheer me up.'

'There are so many stories about home,' the little girl sighed.

'Then tell me your favourite.' Namaan's wife crushed marjoram and thyme between her fingers, and stirred them into the oils.

'The best stories are the ones about Elisha, the prophet,' the little girl said. 'He's very famous, but I'm a bit scared of him. Do you know what he did to the cheeky children? He was going through a new village one day and some naughty children ran after him shouting, "Clear off, Baldy! Baldy! Shiny-top!" and Elisha the prophet turned round and glared at them and called two bears out of the woods. Out they came, as big as trees, and bowed down to him. And do you know what the bears did next?' Her eyes were round and solemn. She dropped her voice to a whisper. 'They ate forty-two of the children!'

Her mistress smiled. 'And I expect your mother told you never to go near Elisha the prophet!'

'She did! But she said he's a good man. He travels round from town to town with his other prophet friends and he helps people. Once he put salt in a spring of foul water and made it pure enough to drink. He's very clever.'

'Mmm,' said her mistress. 'I suppose that was quite clever.'

'I know an even better story about him,' the little slave girl said. 'One of his prophet friends died and the widow came to Elisha and said that she hadn't got anything to live on. The ministers of the government wanted to take her two sons away from her, and guess what Elisha told her to do?'

Namaan's wife tweaked the little girl's ear. 'I can't imagine, but I'm sure you'll tell me anyway. But make the bread while you're doing it.'

The little girl dipped her hand into the flour jar. 'He asked her what she had in the house, and she said, one pot, with just a bit of oil in it, that's all I have. After that, there's nothing.' The child lifted her mistress's oil pot and poured a little oil into the flour and kneaded it. 'So Elisha said, "Easy. Send those boys of yours out and get them to beg every pot they can find, empty or full, it doesn't matter. And fill all the empty pots from your pot." So she did, and sure enough, there was plenty of oil in her pot for all the other pots, and she kept sending the boys out for more till there wasn't a pot left in town. And she filled those up too! By this time, of course, nobody else had any oil—it was all in the widow's kitchen, pots and all. And Elisha said, "Now you can sell all these pots of oil to your neighbours, and you'll never be poor again, right?" '

'That was very helpful,' Namaan's wife agreed. 'Put wood in the oven, child, and get that bread baking.'

The little girl ran outside and came back with an armful of sticks. 'Oh, and another thing Elisha did. This was when the king of Moab was trying to invade Israel.' She was still chattering away while she was snapping the sticks and pushing them under the oven. 'The king of Israel sent for Elisha to help him. Elisha asked a minstrel to play for him and the music put him in a kind of trance, my mother said. He went like this, look.' The girl made her eyes go dreamy. 'And then he told our king to dig lots of ditches across the battlefield, and they filled up with water even though there was a drought. When the sun came up the water looked like blood, and the king of Moab thought all he had to do was to march in and take Israel because the Israelites were all dead. Victory is ours, he cheered! But the kings of Israel and Edom and Judah and all their soldiers were waiting for him. He soon found out that you can't beat Israel!'

'I'm sure you're right,' said her mistress sadly. Syria had raided Israel many times, and her husband had brought home rich spoils, but what good had it done him? It didn't stop him getting leprosy. He was wasting away, day by day. He was grotesque to look at. Already he had lost the use of both his hands, and he was getting worse. He had been the best soldier in the country, and nobody wanted anything to do with him any more. What good had war done him?

'Help me prepare more oil for your master,' she said wearily. 'It won't cure him, but it soothes him. There's nothing else we can do for him.'

'I could take him to Elisha,' the little girl suggested. 'He can do so many things! He can cure people. There was a woman who couldn't have any children, and he told her she would have a son, and she did! It's true!'

'She must have been very happy,' sighed her mistress. 'Bring me more healing herbs, child, and we'll rub them into the oils.'

Still chattering, the little girl ran from the lavender bush to the lemon balm, and brought back armfuls of sweet-smelling sprigs. 'But then something terrible happened,' she went on. 'The woman's little boy died! He just fell on his knees and died. And Elisha picked him up in his arms and put him on a bed and lay across him and breathed on him, just like the great prophet Elijah did, and the boy CAME BACK TO LIFE! Honestly. Oh please, mistress, tell my lord Namaan to go to Elisha. Please.'

The mistress and the little girl went to Namaan with the healing oils and found him hunched up in his room. This fine strong man who had been the greatest soldier in the whole of Syria could hardly move his arms or his legs any more. His body was slowly being eaten away.

'Please!' said the little girl, 'tell him about Elisha.'

And so Namaan's wife told him all the stories about Elisha, and begged him to journey to Samaria and seek him out.

'The king of Israel would throw me out. He hates the Syrians,' Namaan said. 'Why should he lend me his prophet?'

'Elisha's not the king's prophet,' said the little girl. 'He doesn't work for the king, he works for the God of Israel. Oh, please ask him to help you.'

Well, Namaan was in despair of ever finding a cure, so he decided to give Elisha a try. It couldn't do him any harm. He went to the king of Syria and asked for permission to travel into Israel to seek the prophet

Elisha. The king ordered silver and gold and ten changes of clothing to be sent with Namaan, so the king of Israel would know that he was coming in peace, not in war. And Namaan's wife sent her little slave girl, to give her a chance to see Israel again.

The king of Israel refused to accept the gifts, however, or to send for Elisha.

'Who do you think I am? A giver of life and death?' He was so angry that he ripped his own clothes in half.

Namaan turned away. 'Well, that's that,' he said. 'I knew it would be like this. There's no hope for me now.'

'But there is,' whispered the little girl. 'Look at that man running towards us. It's Gehazi, Elisha's servant. I know it is.'

Sure enough, Elisha had heard about the great warrior who was being eaten away by leprosy, whose skin was covered in white scales that flaked away to nothing, and he had sent his servant to see what he could do for him. Gehazi eyed up all the silver and gold and fine clothes that the king of Israel had refused, and he rubbed his hands together.

'Will Elisha come to see me?' Namaan asked.

'No,' said Gehazi. 'There's no need for him to see you.'

Namaan was annoyed. 'He's not much of a healer, if he can't even be bothered to step out of his door to visit the sick. I'm going back to Syria.'

'Oh please,' said the little girl. 'Listen to Gehazi.'

Gehazi eyed the bags of gold lovingly. 'Elisha says if you dip yourself seven times in the River Jordan, you'll be cured.'

'The River Jordan!' shouted Namaan. 'What kind of a prophet is this? We've plenty of fine rivers where I come from; why should I go and paddle in the muddy River Jordan, of all places?'

Once more he turned his horse for home, and once more the little girl pleaded with him.

'What did you want him to say, master? If he asked you to climb the highest mountain, would that do? If he asked you to kill a lion with your bare hands, would that do? Try what he says. It won't do any harm. Please.'

So, grumbling with annoyance, Namaan turned his horse and headed for the River Jordan. He waded in and dipped under the water seven times, and all the silvery flakes sailed away from him. His skin was firm and healed. He was cured.

He rode as fast as he could to the simple little hut where Elisha lived. The little slave girl peered out from under the covers on the waggon, half afraid and half in awe of the famous prophet. It was true, he was completely bald, but she said nothing.

Namaan climbed down and went on his knees to thank him.

'Go on your knees to God, not to me,' said Elisha.

'Then please take your reward,' Namaan said. 'I've brought silver and gold for you, and fine garments. Take it all.'

Elisha shook his head. 'What use is silver and gold and fine garments to a prophet of God?' he asked. 'I've no need of stuff like that. Take it back to your king.'

'Can I take something from here?' Namaan asked. 'Can I take two bags of soil from Israel, so I may kneel on it and pray to your God when I am home?'

'My God is your God,' said Elisha.

And Namaan set off for home with his two bags of soil strapped to the sides of his horse.

The little slave girl rode with him, thrilled to have seen the great prophet and not to have been eaten by bears. She couldn't wait to go back to Syria and tell her mistress. But they had hardly travelled more than a mile when they heard a pounding on the earth behind them, and they turned to see Elisha's servant Gehazi racing after them.

'Namaan! Namaan!' he panted. 'Elisha has sent me to ask if he could have the reward after all.'

The little girl stared at him, very surprised, but Gehazi went on, 'Two young prophets have just come down from the mountains with nothing, nothing at all, and he wants to give them something.'

'Of course he can have it,' Namaan said. 'Take as much as you can carry.' And he heaped the bags into Gehazi's arms.

Then Namaan and the little girl went on their way, back to Syria.

Gehazi stumbled back to the house with his burden of gold and silver and fine garments. He dug a hole under his mattress and hid the lot in the sand. 'Mine, mine, all mine!' he crowed.

When he had cleaned himself up he went and stood before Elisha and asked him if he needed anything before sleeping that night.

Elisha looked at his servant gravely. 'Yes,' he said. 'I do, Gehazi. I need to know where you've been.'

'Me? Been? Oh, nowhere in particular,' Gehazi mumbled.

The great prophet Elisha sighed. 'Don't lie to me, Gehazi. My heart went with you this afternoon. I know very well where you went, and what you have done. You have taken the reward of Namaan and kept it for yourself. Well, you will take his disease too. Stretch out your hand.'

Gehazi stretched out his hand, and saw that his skin was covered in silvery white scales that flaked into dust at his feet.

'You will be a leper for the rest of your life, and so will your children and so will their children, until the end of time.'

And the slave girl heard the end of that story many years later, and told it to the children of Namaan the warrior and his wife, and to all their children too.

Jezebel

Before he died, Elisha sent one of the younger prophets to Gilead. His task was to anoint Jehu, son of Jehoshaphat, as king of Israel in place of King Joram.

Jehu was surprised to see the prophet, who had ridden furiously and arrived with dishevelled hair and dusty skin in the middle of a feast, but, being polite to visitors, he did as he was requested and went to speak to him privately in a quiet room. To his astonishment, the young prophet asked him to kneel in front of him, then brought out a phial of holy oil and anointed him.

'You are now the king of Israel,' he said. 'But you must avenge Elisha for all the wrongs that Ahab has done against his prophets.' He told Jehu what he must do, and then as he left him, he said, 'You must get rid of Joram and Ahaziah. And above all, Jezebel must die. Death is too good for her; the dogs in the street will tear her to pieces and eat her flesh.' And he ran out, wild with anger.

The guests at the feast laughed when Jehu returned. 'What did that holy madman want?' they asked.

'He came from Elisha,' Jehu said. 'He has made me king of Israel.'

The people took off their cloaks at once and laid them on the bare tiles around Jehu, as a sign of respect, but Jehu didn't tell them what he had been asked to do. He would never forget what the prophet had said, that he must take revenge on Ahab and Jezebel. When he was ready, he gathered his men around him and rode across the country with a kind of fury inside him, and news of his coming galloped ahead of him and spread fear in the hearts of all the enemies of Israel. First he approached Joram, who sent a messenger to meet him.

'Is it peace?' the horseman shouted, and Jehu called back, 'What have you to do with peace? Join my men, and fight at my side.'

When the horseman did not return, Joram sent another. 'Is it peace?' the horseman called, and again Jehu answered, 'What have you to do with peace? Fall in behind me.'

'They're not coming back,' a watchman told Joram. 'They've fallen in with Jehu—you should see him, he's riding like a man gone crazy!'

So King Joram of Israel and King Ahaziah of Judah rode out together to meet Jehu, and called to him, 'Is it peace, Jehu?'

'How can there be peace when men like you and wicked women like Jezebel remain alive?'

The two men reined in their horses and turned to flee in terror, and Jehu drew his bow and shot them.

That done, Jehu rode on to Jezreel. He had only completed half of the task that Elisha had set him. Jezebel heard that he was coming, and she put make-up on her face and piled up her hair, glittered herself with jewels, and smiled down at Jehu and his horsemen from her window.

'Is it peace?' she called down.

Jehu ignored her. 'Is anyone on my side against this woman of sin?' he shouted.

Two of Jezebel's servants ran forward at once, lifted her out of her chair and threw her out of the window. Her blood spattered the walls as she fell, and the horses trampled her to death. Jehu did nothing to help her. He watched her die, then went indoors to dine. When he had finished his meal he said to one of his men, 'After all, she was the daughter of a king. Give her a royal burial.'

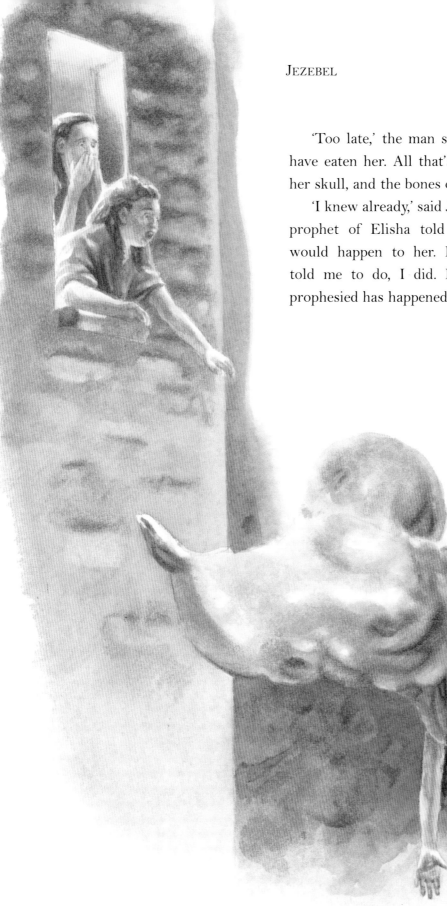

JEZEBEL

'Too late,' the man said. 'The dogs have eaten her. All that's left of her is her skull, and the bones of her hands.'

'I knew already,' said Jehu. 'The mad prophet of Elisha told me that this would happen to her. Everything he told me to do, I did. Everything he prophesied has happened.'

Daniel and Nebuchadnezzar

For a long time, after King Jehu died, the people of Israel went back to worshipping false gods. Now was the time for their punishment. God removed them from his sight because of the sins of their king, Jeraboam. He let them be conquered by the huge Assyrian army and taken away by the thousands into Syria. There they lived in exile, estranged from their homeland.

Judah alone resisted the attackers, and stood firm. Jerusalem, the beautiful city of David, remained untouched by the invaders. A young Jewish prince called Daniel lived there with his friends Hananiah, Mishael, and Azariah, and every day they worshipped at the gorgeous temple which had been built long ago by Solomon. God lived there. He had breathed his spirit into it, and he had stayed there. At last it seemed that the Jews, the descendents of the Hebrew slaves, were settled in their holy place.

But peace is always broken. There is always war and greed and hatred. This time it was the king of Babylon, rich and powerful though he was, who wanted more. He wanted Judah, the land of the Jews. He sent his armies marching across the land; they burnt every building, they plundered every house, and whenever they found anything that was worth keeping, they took it for Nebuchadnezzar's treasury. What they did not want, they destroyed.

As they advanced towards the holy city of Jerusalem itself, Daniel and his friends were watching from the ramparts. They couldn't believe what was happening to their country, but they were sure that Jerusalem was safe. It was surrounded by thick, high walls and massive gates. It was impenetrable. From all over Judah people fled to the holy city with their carts and chariots piled with their meagre belongings. They drove their cattle ahead of them, their mules and horses, their sheep and camels, and they herded them all inside the city gates. Then the gates were closed behind them. All they could do now was wait.

But Nebuchadnezzar was happy to wait too. When his army reached the city the soldiers surrounded it and set up camp there. Daniel and his friends and the other boys of Jerusalem jeered from the ramparts.

'We're safe here!' they shouted. 'You can't do any harm to us now.'

But the older people knew well that Nebuchadnezzar's weapon against them was not going to be swords or stones or knives. It was going to be the greatest enemy known to man: hunger.

For two years the soldiers stayed in their camp. For two years the people hung on inside the city; cramped, afraid, and hungry. Before long they had eaten all their stored food. They had eaten all the figs and dates and nuts on the trees. They had eaten all the animals. They were starving. They ate the grass on the ground. They boiled belts and skins to make soup from the leather. They were weak and helpless. And when he knew that there was no fight left in them, Nebuchadnezzar ordered the people in Jerusalem to open the gates, and they did. His soldiers marched in and took the city. They set it on fire, and they destroyed the holy, wonderful temple of Solomon, where God himself lived.

'They've killed God!' the people sobbed.

And then Daniel knew his own power and wisdom. 'God cannot be killed,' he said. 'God lives in us.'

Anyone who was fit enough to walk was taken to Babylon to serve King Nebuchadnezzar. The rest were left to die in the ruins of Jerusalem.

So it happened that Daniel came to Babylon. He and Hananiah, Mishael, and Azariah were marched there, and it seemed to them that nothing worse could happen to them. After days of marching, weak and hungry and despairing, Daniel saw ahead of him the place that was to be his new home: Babylon, the gorgeous city that Nebuchadnezzar had built for himself, with its golden temple perched on top of a ziggurat a hundred metres high, its sumptuous palace with gardens hanging like green waterfalls, all reflected in the blue waters of the Euphrates.

'This is beautiful,' he said to his friends. 'If this is to be our home, we must be princes here.'

As they approached the gates he could see that the walls were decorated with blue enamelled tiles depicting bulls and deer and wild creatures of the mountains. He paused by one that had a lion enamelled into it, and he touched it, tracing the outline with his finger, fascinated.

'Come on,' a soldier said roughly. 'Get moving!'

Daniel looked at his friends. 'Don't be afraid,' he said. 'I'm not.'

Every day Jews went down to the waters of Babylon and wept for their homeland, for the lost city of Jerusalem. Daniel tried to comfort them and to encourage them to make the most of their captivity.

'We will go back,' he told them. 'One day the Jews will return to Jerusalem. But while we're here, we must be strong and brave.'

Nebuchadnezzar noticed how the Jewish prisoners listened to Daniel, and he realized that the young prince was a clever man. He and his friends were strong and good-looking, and so the king decided that he would have them trained for special duties in his court. They were given new names: Hananiah was renamed Shadrach, Mishael was called Meshach, and Azariah was called Abednego. Daniel was given the name of Belteshazzar, close to the name of the king's own son, Balshazzar. But among his own people he was always known as Daniel.

The four princes were to be taught the Chaldean literature and language of Babylon, and they were given special privileges. Every day the rich food that was served to the king's courtiers was brought to them, but they refused it.

'We were starved for two whole years, and we survived,' Daniel said to the others. 'We don't need their meat, because it's not prepared in our way. We'll eat the simple food of the peasants, pulses and grains from the earth, and they'll see how we will prosper.'

The four princes soon became the king's favourites at court, which did not please the other court officials. The young men were quick, wise, clever, and handsome, just the sort of men that a king likes to have around him. But he did not yet know how great a power they had.

One night King Nebuchadnezzar had a dream, which he couldn't understand. He sent for his enchanters and magicians and said, 'Tell me what I dreamt last night, and what it means. If you can, I'll reward you. If you can't, I'll kill you.'

'How can we interpret your dream if we can't know what it is?' the chief magician reasoned with him, but Nebuchadnezzar flew into a passionate rage and told them that they would all be torn limb from limb for their ignorance and stupidity. As soon as Daniel heard about this he went to the king and asked him to be merciful to the enchanters.

'Can you do any better?' the king demanded.

'No man can,' Daniel answered, showing no fear. 'No wise man or enchanter or magician on earth can tell you what your dream was.'

'Pah! You're as bad as the rest of them,' Nebuchadnezzar roared.

'I can't tell you, but God can,' Daniel went on. 'God can tell you the secret of your dream. You saw a huge statue. The head was made of gold. The body was made of silver, and bronze, and iron, and the feet were made of clay. And a stone broke the statue into pieces, and it all blew away like dust in the air. And the stone became a mountain that covered the earth.'

'You're right,' said the king, amazed. 'That's exactly what I dreamt.' He leaned forward, tapping his sceptre on the patterned floor. 'Ah, but can you tell me what it means?'

'God can,' Daniel said. 'You have seen into the future. You are a mighty king, and you are the statue's head of gold. Those limbs of silver and bronze and iron and clay are the lesser nations that will follow yours. And the stone that destroys them is the hand of God, who is greater than anything.'

Nebuchadnezzar was so impressed that he went down on his knees in front of Daniel. He made him ruler of the whole province of Babylon, and he gave his three friends, Shadrach, Meshach, and Abednego, positions of great power. But they never forgot that they were princes of Judah, and that their God was with them still.

To show how much the dream had meant to him, Nebuchadnezzar had a huge golden statue built. When it was finished he held a ceremony to show the statue to all his people. He brought musicians together, drummers and harpists and trumpeters, and ordered everyone to worship this idol. Daniel remained in the court, but Shadrach, Meshach, and Abednego were present at the ceremony, and they all refused to go on their knees and worship Nebuchadnezzar's god.

'Do it, or you will be thrown in the fiery furnace,' Nebuchadnezzar raged, and still they refused. Nebuchadnezzar's face was as purple as thunder. These men, who had been dragged from a fallen city and given all the privileges of courtiers, these Jews who had been made governors of his kingdom, dared to disobey him in front of his subjects.

'Make the furnace seven times hotter than usual,' he roared. 'Bind their legs and arms so they can't move, and throw them in.'

The furnace was so hot that the servants who had to bind the three princes and throw them into the flames were overcome by the heat and perished. But when Nebuchadnezzar looked down into the pit he saw Shadrach, Meshach, and Abednego walking in the flames as if they were strolling along the banks of the Euphrates on a cool day.

There was a fourth person with them: an angel with folded wings that shimmered like starlight. Nebuchadnezzar could not believe what he was seeing. He ordered the princes to be pulled out of the furnace, and they stood before him. Nothing was damaged. Their skin was perfect, their hair was not scorched, and they didn't even smell of smoke. But there was no more sign of the angel.

'Your God is my God now,' Nebuchadnezzar declared. 'No other god will be worshipped in this country. No other god could do this thing. Anyone who refuses to worship him will be thrown on the dung-heap.'

But Nebuchadnezzar soon fell back into his old ways of worshipping false gods, and some time later he had another dream that frightened him. He sent for all his magicians and enchanters, but none of them could interpret his dream. Then he sent for Daniel.

'You are the greatest dream-reader of them all,' he said. 'Tell me what my dream means, because the memory of it is driving me mad. I saw a tree, an enormous almond tree in full blossom, and its branches reached up to the sky. It could be seen from one end of the world to the other. All the animals and birds and insects fed from it and found shelter under it. But while I lay in my bed gazing at this wonderful tree, a voice from heaven ordered the tree to be chopped down; its leaves stripped. All that should be left was the stump. It was watered by the dew, and it turned into an animal for seven years. This is all very strange. Tell me what it means.'

Daniel understood the dream at once, but he was afraid to tell Nebuchadnezzar the terrible truth of it. The king begged him, and at last he said, 'Nebuchadnezzar, you are a great king. You are that great and wonderful tree. But you will be driven away from your family, from your wife, from your son Balshazzar, from all your subjects. You will be driven away from those you love and those you hate, and you will live with the wild animals. You will eat grass, you will be bathed with dew, and you will live like this for seven years until you accept that God is the Lord of all kingdoms.'

Already Nebuchadnezzar could see that his flesh was growing hairy, that his hands were turning into hooves. When he spoke, his voice was a growl of terror. He dropped onto all fours and lumbered like an ox through his own palace doors and out of the gates of Babylon. He tore at the grass with his teeth, and drank the morning dew, and he lived the life of a wild animal for seven years.

Balshazzar's Banquet

Nebuchadnezzar's son Balshazzar immediately became the king. He lived a corrupted life in the palace, feasting and drinking and squandering his father's wealth. Every night he invited princes and lords to banquet with him, and the noise of their feasting and drunkenness echoed round the marbled halls.

Daniel heard it all and knew there was nothing he could do to prevent it. He began to have dreams himself, terrifying and wonderful, which showed the empires of the world as huge, strange monsters. He saw a lion with wings, a bear with tusks, a flying leopard with four heads, and a monster with iron teeth and horns, and all these creatures rose up out of the deep dark sea. In the middle of all these wild beasts a human being stood. Daniel tossed and turned in his bed trying to make sense of the dream, and at last an angel spoke to him and said: 'The beasts are the evil kingdoms of the world, which bring chaos and destruction. The wicked will always be wicked, and there is no reward for them. But the good people who are the children of Abraham and Isaac and Moses will receive the kingdom of Israel and bless it for ever and ever. Rest now, Daniel, and your reward will come at the end of your days.'

Daniel slept peacefully at last, but he was woken up by one of Balshazzar's servants. The man was very frightened, and said Daniel was to come at once to the banqueting hall, because Balshazzar was about to go mad with fear.

Balshazzar had invited a thousand lords to a feast in the great blue-tiled hall of the palace. They had eaten more than their stomachs could hold, and drunk more than their heads could bear. Balshazzar had sent for the altarpieces, the golden chalice and platters that King Nebuchadnezzar's army had stolen from Solomon's temple in Jerusalem before they destroyed it. Now he poured wine into the chalice and passed it round as if it were a common everyday vessel and not a sacred object intended for religious rites. And as soon as his fat lips touched the precious chalice, strange writing appeared on the wall behind his head, scribbled by a human hand with no body attached to it. The lords screamed with fear; they covered their eyes, and when they looked again they could see words that meant nothing at all:

MENE MENE (ⵣⵉⵙ ⵣⵉⵙ)

TEKEL

UPHARSIN

Balshazzar yelled for his magicians to come and interpret the words, but none of them could. And that was when he sent for Daniel.

'Tell me what this means, and you can have anything you want—gold, jewels, a purple cloak like mine, a crown, anything.' He was shaking with fear.

'Keep your reward,' Daniel said. 'Have you learnt nothing from your father? There he is, thrown out of his own palace, living with the beasts out in the fields, no shelter, no comfort. He is being punished for thinking that he was better than God, but what you are doing is even worse. You are drinking from holy vessels. You worship false gods of gold and silver. These gods are worthless. The God who breathed life into you is the only God. This is what these words mean: MENE MENE: your kingdom is finished. TEKEL: you have sinned. UPHARSIN: your kingdom is torn in two.'

And that night, Balshazzar was slain.

Daniel and the Lions

So now there was a new king and his name was Darius. He was determined to rule the kingdom differently, and he divided it into one hundred and twenty parts, each governed by a different president. This was very fair and it was a good idea, because it put a lot of men in positions of power. But he made one great mistake. Because he liked and admired Daniel so much, he put him in the highest position of all, over all the other presidents. Naturally, they were jealous and angry. They hated Daniel, and they did their best to find fault with him so the king would take his power away. But it was impossible; Daniel was faultless. He prayed to God three times a day, he was thoughtful and kind to his friends and courteous to his enemies. The king loved him because he was perfect in every way, and the one hundred and twenty presidents hated him for the same reason.

'There's only one way we can find fault with this man,' they decided. 'It will have be something to do with God.'

At last they came up with an idea. They went to the king and said that they had come up with a new ruling which would show the kingdom how mighty Darius was.

'How will you do that?' he asked, though secretly he was flattered and hoped there would be a way.

'For thirty days no one should be allowed to pray to anyone,' the spokesman said. 'Not to anyone at all, divine or human, except to the king himself. If anyone disobeys, they must be thrown to the lions.'

The king thought it was a wonderful idea, and he signed the document that the conspirators thrust into his hands, and sealed it with a kiss from his ring.

'This law can't be changed for thirty days, remember,' they said, and the king nodded.

Daniel heard about the law, but thought nothing of it at all. He was not going to change his ways for a rule that made no sense to him. There was only one person to pray to, and that was God. The windows of his house faced towards his ravaged city of Jerusalem, where the fallen temple of Solomon lay in ruins. Three times a day he went up to his room, opened his window, and prayed. Nothing was going to stop him.

As soon as the conspirators saw him praying they hurried to the king, excited because their plan had worked. 'Daniel has broken the law,' they said. 'He prays to his God, not to you.'

King Darius was horrified. 'Daniel is above the law,' he said. 'I excuse him.'

'No, there are no excuses,' the men said. 'The law is the law, and Daniel has broken it. You signed the document yourself; you sealed it with your own ring. Daniel must be thrown in the lion's den.'

In great distress the king himself went to Daniel and told him what had happened. 'May your God preserve you,' he said. He went back to his palace and stayed awake all night, not eating, not sleeping, in a torment of fear and shame.

The lions were very hungry. One hundred and twenty presidents had seen to that. They paced and growled round their den, snarling at each other, snarling at the voices of men up above them, snarling at the flickering torches of the approaching guards, and at their loud taunting voices. The stone that guarded the entrance to the den was rolled back and Daniel was thrown inside. The stone was rolled to behind him, and the guard and the conspirators ran upstairs to the gallery to watch the fun.

Daniel's heart was pounding, his limbs were faint with fear, yet he stood upright and faced the lions. They circled him slowly, soundless now except for the padding of their great paws. Round and round him they went, nudging each other, their jaws open and dripping, and they never took their eyes off Daniel.

He remembered his dream. He remembered the beasts that rose from the sea, and the man who rose among them. That man was the good man who would be blessed for ever, and would receive his reward in heaven. He remembered how he and his people had been marched away from their holy city and brought to Babylon, years ago, and he thought of himself standing outside the blue walls looking at the enamelled tiles with their pictures of lions. He held out his hand, and he touched one of the lions.

And the den was filled with the golden light of an angel.

As soon as it was daylight King Darius hurried down to the lions' den. He knew he would find a terrible sight of blood and bones strewn around it.

'Daniel, oh, Daniel,' he wept at the stone outside the den. 'I am sorry for what I have done to you.'

To his amazement Daniel's voice answered him, 'Long live King Darius!'

'He's alive!' the king gasped. 'Let everyone worship his God.'

The stone was rolled back, and Daniel walked out, untouched.

But the men who had plotted against him, and their wives, and their children, their cousins, and their servants, were all thrown to the lions and torn to pieces, so great was the fury of King Darius of Babylon.

Esther, the Queen of Persia

If it hadn't been for a well-kept secret, all the Jews in Persia would have died. This is the story.

Xerxes ruled the mighty kingdom of Persia, which stretched all the way from India in the east to Ethiopia in the west. He was wealthy beyond dreams, and he loved to show off his magnificent palace with all its gorgeous mosaics and marble pillars. He held an exhibition there in Susa and invited all the most powerful men of his kingdom to come and see it for themselves, and to marvel at his treasure house of jewels and gold and silver ornaments. At the end of the exhibition, which lasted six months, he held a banquet for the people of Susa. The banquet lasted seven days, and was the most luxurious affair anyone in that city had ever attended. There was enough food and wine for the whole of Persia, never mind for the citizens of Susa. The only thing missing was the Queen of Persia.

Her name was Vashti. She held a banquet of her own in the women's house, but she was also expected to put in an appearance at Xerxes's banquet, so he could show her off. She was very beautiful. He wanted her to sit at his side with all her sparkling rubies and emeralds and be admired by everyone. But she refused to come. He sent for her seven times, and every time she had a different excuse: she was tired, she had a headache, she wanted to read, she wanted to bathe, she needed to have her hair dressed, she had friends visiting; she simply did not want to come.

King Xerxes was furious. Her refusal made him look small and foolish in front of his subjects. They must all be laughing at him. In spite of all the wealth and luxury of his court, the king had a wife who would not obey him.

'Enough is enough. Tell her I never want to see her again,' he shouted to his servants. 'She's banished from my court for ever.'

When they ran to her with his message, Vashti took her favourite dresses and a few servants and left the palace, and was never seen or heard of again. King Xerxes turned to the only person he could trust, his chief adviser, Haman.

'Every man should be master in his own house,' he said gloomily. 'I did the right thing, didn't I, Haman? Ah, but I'm lonely without her.'

'Find yourself a new queen,' Haman advised him. 'It doesn't do for the king to be seen alone.'

Xerxes brightened up. 'That's a good idea,' he said. 'I can have anyone I want. I can have someone younger and even more beautiful than Vashti.'

'Let the people see that you always have the best of everything,' Haman said.

'That's it. Go and find me the most beautiful woman in Persia, and I'll have her for my wife.'

So Haman led a search for the most beautiful women who could be found. A hundred women were brought to the court for the king to choose from. Among them was a Jewish girl called Esther. She was an orphan from a family of exiled Jews and she had been brought up by her uncle Mordecai.

'The king won't want me,' she said to her uncle. 'He would never choose a Jewish woman for his wife. We don't even belong here.'

'Then don't tell him you're Jewish,' Mordecai advised her. 'He'll never know if you don't tell him. Give yourself a chance to better yourself, Esther. If you do become queen you would be the most powerful Jewish woman in the world. Remember that.'

For twelve months Esther had to live in the house of women with all the other candidates. They all had to be purified with perfumed oils before they were shown to the king. The male servants who looked after them showed them how to redden their cheeks with mulberry juice, and how to make their eyes shine by brushing the lids round them with black kohl. They taught them how to gather rose petals and drop them into hot oil to make a perfume, which would scent their bodies with irresistible sweetness.

At last Esther was sent for. Nobody guessed that she was a Jewish refugee, and she looked so beautiful that Xerxes fell in love with her at once. She was graceful and gentle and meek and everything a wife should be. He had a crown made especially for her, and it was thickly crusted with topaz and amethyst, with pearls and with rubies. On the day of the wedding everyone in Persia had a day's holiday. Another banquet was held, and this time the king had his wife at his side for everyone to admire. And still Esther kept her secret.

Every day her uncle Mordecai sat outside the palace gates to catch a glimpse of her. He had brought her to Persia as a homeless child, her parents had been killed when Israel was conquered; she had nothing. And now she was the queen of Persia. And it was while he was sitting there one day that he overheard two of the royal servants plotting to assassinate the king. He sent a message straight away to Esther, and she came to the gates to see him.

'What is it, uncle?' she asked.

'The king has two servants called Bigthan and Teresh,' he told her. 'They are making plans to attack him in the night and stab him to death. You must warn him, Esther.'

This wasn't easy, even when the message was so urgent. If Esther tried to go into the king's court without his permission she would be killed outright. She had to wait to be sent for, and then she had to stand in the doorway of the inner court waiting for Xerxes to lift his golden sceptre, which was the sign that she could enter. Luckily he was so in love with her still that he wanted to be with her all the time, and as soon as he saw her in the doorway he lifted his sceptre.

'You have two servants called Bigthan and Teresh,' she said.

'I do. But what business is that of yours?' he asked her.

'Listen, my lord. They're planning to kill you during the night.'

'What makes you think that?' he asked, teasing her a little to hide his alarm.

'They were overheard by a man called Mordecai.' Esther didn't tell the king that Mordecai was her uncle. He was known to be a Jew, and she still had her secret to keep.

The king sent orders immediately for Bigthan and Teresh to be hanged from the gallows outside the palace gates. It was important that his subjects should see the hanging, so they would know how severely he ruled his kingdom.

King Xerxes was very pleased with Esther, and even more pleased with Haman, who had advised him to get a new wife in the first place. He made him the chief of all his servants. Haman wanted to make sure that all the people of Susa were aware of his importance, and so he made a public appearance at the palace gates. Everyone bowed down to him, except Mordecai, who was waiting as usual for a sight of Esther. When the guards asked him why he wouldn't bow to Haman, he said, 'Why should I? I'm Jewish. He's not one of my people.'

Nothing could have made Haman more angry. 'Jews don't belong in Persia,' he said. 'It's time we got rid of you, all of you.'

Still angry, he went to the king to tell him his thoughts. 'There are some people in your kingdom who shouldn't be here,' he said. 'They're scattered here and there all over the place, but they have no right to be here. They don't respect our laws, they don't respect our government, and they don't respect you. I advise you to get rid of them.'

King Xerxes was grateful for his advice, as always. His subjects must be obedient to him—if they weren't, they were a danger to the state.

'Your advice is always faultless,' he said. 'What would I do without you? Here, take my ring and use it to seal any orders you send out about these bothersome people. I leave it all to you.'

In no time Haman had letters written out and sealed with the stamp of the royal ring, so everyone would know that the orders came directly from the king himself. He sent them out to all the provinces of Persia, to be posted up in public places, to be read aloud to all the king's subjects. And the letters caused terror in every Jewish quarter of Persia. This is what they said:

By order of King Xerxes, the Jewish people are to be exterminated on the thirteenth day of the twelfth month of this year. Let not a man, woman, or child remain alive, if they are of Jewish families. Let all their possessions be seized, and let every Jew be killed.

Throughout Persia the Jewish people sent up a wail of despair. Why was the king treating them so cruelly when they had done nothing wrong? Were they always to be haunted and hunted in this way?

It was the most terrible thing imaginable. It was bad enough to be driven from one country to another; it was bad enough to be sold as slaves. Now they were to be exterminated; the entire Jewish population of Persia would be wiped out. Many of them travelled to Susa to sit outside the gates of the king's palace, desperate for a chance to ask him why he was planning to do this to them. They had done nothing to deserve it. Mordecai told them to dress themselves in coarse sackcloth and rub ash on their faces, as a sign of mourning for the Jewish people. And every time Haman saw Mordecai he smiled with contempt.

'This will reward you for your insolence,' he snarled. 'This will reward you for being Jewish.'

Esther was in a torment when she realized what was happening. Her uncle sent her a message to say she must speak to her husband, and she sent a message back to say that the king had not sent for her or granted her permission to enter his inner court. She was powerless. Again Mordecai sent her a message.

'Even though you are the queen of Persia, you are still a Jew.'

Esther knew then that it was time for her to reveal her secret, though it put her own life in terrible danger. She fasted for three days to prepare herself, praying to God to give her the courage to do what was right. At the end of the three days she walked towards the inner court, determined to ignore the guards and to walk right in.

If he kills me, he kills me, she thought. I'll die anyway, when he finds out that I'm Jewish.

But the king had been missing her company. When he saw her standing at the door of the court he smiled and raised his golden sceptre, signalling at her to come in. He had not left the palace for days—the noise of the wailing supplicants at his gates was too much for him. Beautiful Esther would lighten his heart and his spirits.

'What do you want, my love?' he asked her. 'Even if you ask for half my kingdom, I will give it to you.'

She smiled sweetly at him, though she was trembling inside. 'I want to hold a banquet in my house for you and for your adviser, Haman.'

Haman was delighted when the invitation was sent to him. He

boasted about it to his wife and to all his friends.

'She hasn't invited anyone else,' he told them. 'Just me and his majesty. She thinks very highly of me.'

'You must be the happiest man in the world,' his friends said.

'Nearly,' Haman replied. He had just caught sight of the man he hated more than all the Jews put together, the man who refused to bow to him: Mordecai.

'I can't even wait till the thirteenth day to get rid of that man,' he said to himself. He ordered the guards to erect a high gallows at the gates for everyone to see. 'Before the week is out, Mordecai will be hanged,' he smiled. 'Then I'll be the happiest man in the world. I'll go to the queen's banquet, and everyone will know how important I am.'

The king was restless that night; even in his gorgeous palace he couldn't escape from the ceaseless lamentations of the Jews pleading at his gates. It was impossible to sleep through it all. In the end he gave up trying to sleep and sent for his secretary to read out the court diary of recent events. When the secretary came to the bit about the hanging of Bigthan and Teresh, his traitorous servants, Xerxes remembered that he had never rewarded Mordecai for warning him and saving his life. He decided to ask Haman's advice about it.

Morning came. Most of the Jews were sleeping at the gates, exhausted, but Mordecai was still on his knees praying for God to help them.

'Be quick with those gallows!' Haman shouted to the guards, and hurried to the king to arrange for the hanging.

'Your majesty, do I have your permission to hang an insolent chap who refuses to bow to me?' he asked.

'Of course,' said the king. 'Whoever is insolent to you is insolent to me. But before you go, I wish to discuss something much more pleasant with you. It's a matter of reward.'

'Reward, your majesty?' Haman was a little flustered. Was the king thinking of rewarding him for his service? How fitting that would be!

'One of my subjects deserves the highest reward for his loyal service to me. What do you suggest, Haman?'

Haman blushed. No one could have been more loyal to the king than he himself, after all. He knew that, and the king knew that. So he was to choose his own reward? Really, the king relied on him for everything; it was most touching.

'Nothing but the best will do,' he said, bowing slightly. 'I would clothe him in richly patterned garments that you yourself have worn. I have a particular turquoise robe in mind that is most fetching. I would mount him on your own favourite steed—the black Arab stallion, very handsome. And,' his eyes shone, 'I should put a royal crown on his head; the one that is studded with emeralds and diamonds. This most loyal subject of yours should ride through the streets of Susa, so every one of your majesty's subjects will bow down and honour him. Trumpets sounding, a boy's choir, and a host of dancing slaves would lead the way.'

'Excellent!' said the king. 'Your advice always pleases me. Go and make the arrangements, Haman. The man's name is Mordecai.'

'Mordecai!' Haman covered his face in shame and slowly went out to give the orders.

'This Mordecai will be your downfall,' his wife said to him when he told her.

'Nonsense,' said Haman, cheering up already. 'Tomorrow he will be hanged on those gallows outside the gates, so what use will the king's reward be to him? What's more, he goes to his death knowing that all his people will be exterminated on the thirteenth day because of his insolence to me! What does that make him?'

It makes you a monster, his wife thought, but she daren't say it. Nobody dared say anything to anger Haman.

'Besides,' said Haman. 'I'm still the king's favourite. No one else is going to his wife's banquet, remember.'

But his wife shook her head and said nothing.

After the banquet, when Haman and Xerxes were drinking wine and Esther was reclining on her golden couch eating figs, the king said, 'Esther, this has been a very fine banquet. Is there anything you want me to give you—you know everything I have is yours.'

Now is the time, Esther thought. I must be brave, and now is the time.

'There is only one thing I want,' she said. 'I want my life.'

'Your life?' The king laughed, puzzled. 'What do you mean, Esther?'

'There is someone who is going to kill me on the thirteenth day of this month. He is sitting next to you at my table.'

The king stared at Esther and then at Haman.

'He has ordered the deaths of the entire Jewish population of your kingdom, and I am one of them.'

The king was so shocked that he left the room and went out into his garden to think. He had no idea that he had married a Jew. He did not understand the Jews, or the Hebrew God that they worshipped, or the feasts that they held sacred. These were the people who were crouching by his gates in sackcloth and ashes, wailing day and night, day and night. Before long they were to be killed, in his own name. He had been tricked into agreeing to this; he thought getting rid of them meant expelling them from Persia, out of his sight, out of his mind. And he had agreed to this on the advice of his most trusted servant, as close to being a friend as a king could have. But Esther was his wife, and he loved her. Xerxes was deeply troubled by all this, but when at last he went back into the banqueting room he saw Haman flinging himself onto the couch where Esther was lying.

'You dog!' the king roared. 'Would you attack my wife before my eyes? Is there no end to your wickedness?' He called for his guards to take Haman away. 'You deserve the greatest punishment for the greatest treachery,' he said.

Next morning, Haman was hanged from the very gallows that he had prepared for Mordecai. Mordecai was dressed in the king's own robes and rode through the streets on his black Arab mare, to be cheered by all the people of Susa, and all the Jews of the land.

And beautiful Queen Esther, who saved the Persian Jews from extinction, is honoured still for her bravery, and for being one of the most powerful Jewish women the world has ever known.

Jerusalem Rises Again

In that distant land, Nehemiah was weeping. He carried a silver chalice of wine to his master, King Artaxerxes of Persia, as he did every evening, and wept as though his heart would break.

'Tell me,' said the king. 'Are you ill?'

'I have heard that my city is in ruins,' Nehemiah said. 'It was the home of my ancestors, the golden city of the Jewish people, and now it is just a heap of rubble.'

The king nodded gravely. He knew that his predecessor, King Cyrus, had granted all Jews permission to go home if they wanted to, to rebuild the city, and to take with them the treasures that the Babylonians had stolen during the reign of King Nebuchadnezzar.

'May I go there?' Nehemiah asked. 'I want to see for myself. And if it's true, I want to rebuild Jerusalem.'

'Of course you must go,' Artaxerxes said. 'I'll send men to help you, and letters to the governors to give you help with timber and anything else you may need.'

So Nehemiah went to Jerusalem and rode alone through the ruined streets and fallen walls of the great city of David. It was all blackened with fire now.

'With God's help, I can build it again,' he said.

He called together all the old families of the descendants of Jacob, and they came in their thousands to see for themselves. Forty-two thousand three hundred and sixty people came with

their servants and grieved at the devastation of Jerusalem.

'How can those Israelites build a city out of rubble?' some of the outsiders asked. 'The stones are so ruined that a fox would knock the walls down in one jump!'

'If God helps us, we can do it,' Nehemiah said again.

But the Arabs, the Ammonites, and the Ashdodites plotted together to attack Jerusalem and stop the rebuilding of the old city. When Nehemiah heard about the plot he divided his men and women into two halves. He armed one half with picks and shovels and timbers, bolts and bars and nails; they were the workforce, helping the skilled stonemasons to restore the ruined city. He armed the other half with spears and shields, and they stood on guard from the rising of the sun until the stars glittered in the sky. They were the army, and they protected the labourers as they worked. The walls rose up even higher than they had been before. Soon one gateway after another was restored: Fish gate, Dung gate, Sheep gate, Horse gate, Valley gate, East gate, West gate . . .

At last the Jews had their own magnificent city again, and it is said that the whole thing only took fifty-two days.

'With God's help, we have done it,' said Nehemiah.

Jonah and the Monster Fish

You've heard all those stories about God taking revenge on people, drowning them and covering them with boils, and killing all their first-born children. People say he's a jealous god, a vengeful god, that he only loves the Jews and then it's only if they obey him. Maybe now you would like to hear my story.

My name is Jonah, and I'm a Jew. I'm a prophet, so I tell people about God. Sometimes God tells me what to say, and sometimes I know it already from Amittai, my father, and from the old stories. But one day God told me something I didn't want to hear.

Jonah, go to the great city of Nineveh.

I have heard about the wickedness of the people there.

Go and tell them to change their ways.

Nineveh! Well, I did not want to go there. It was miles and miles away from home, for a start, far away in the mountainous country of Assyria. Stories about the lawlessness of its people had reached us in Galilee, and no one would choose to go there—why stick your neck out to have your head chopped off? And they certainly wouldn't be interested in the God of the Jews. So I decided to disobey God. I decided not to go. I ran away to Joppa and when I found a boat setting off for Tarshish I jumped on board quickly, paid my fare, and hid from God.

We were scarcely out of sight of land when fierce gales struck the ship. It reeled like a mad horse, creaking and groaning and flinging its passengers from side to side. I was too ill to move; I went down below deck and rolled myself up in my blanket and lay with my eyes closed while my stomach heaved. I could hear the crew pitching the ship's cargo overboard to make it lighter, but still the ship smashed and wallowed from side to side. I could hear the captain yelling at people to pray to their gods for the gale to stop, or we'd all be drowned. I stayed where I was, but when he saw me lying there he hauled me to my knees.

'How can you sleep through this?' he screamed down my ear. 'Pray to your god, like the rest of us.'

'Somebody has brought this on us,' the sailors were saying. 'If we cast lots, we'll find out who the culprit is for sure.'

Well, they cast lots, and of course the shortest stick drawn was mine, so they knew it was my fault. They gathered round me, shaking me and pulling me to my feet, weak though we all were.

'You must know why this has happened. Who are you? Where are you from?' they all jabbered at me.

So I had to confess. I told them I was a Jew, that I was a prophet, that my God made the sea and he made the dry land, he made everything. And then I told them that I was hiding from him, and that was why the storm had risen, to punish me.

'Then tell him to stop,' they shouted. 'The ship can't hold out much longer. We'll all drown.'

I shook my head. 'He won't listen to me,' I said. 'Throw me overboard, and the storm will stop.' I was so miserable with sea-sickness that I couldn't wait to get off the ship, to tell you the truth. 'Just chuck me overboard.'

'We can't do that,' the captain said. 'We'd be guilty of murder.'

He ordered the men to try to row back to land, but it was impossible; the waves were like mountains.

'Do as I say,' I told him. 'It's all because of me. God only wants to punish me, not you. Throw me overboard, and the storm will stop.'

The captain realized that it was the only chance he had to save the ship and the men on board. They didn't throw me. They lowered me down carefully by my armpits, and as soon as my dangling feet touched the water, the waves grew smaller, but as soon as they started to haul me up again, the waves snapped at their hands. So the captain gave the order to let go, and as I felt the sailors loosening their grip on me and I began to slip away from them, I was more terrified than I have ever been in my life. The sea grew calm, the ship righted itself, but I went down and down, fathoms deep down, down past the mountains that rise under the sea. I floated down away from light into the utter darkness of the ocean, and a great fish loomed up towards me with its jaws open wide like doors, and in I floated.

I was inside the belly of a great monster of a fish: like a whale, but bigger. I could stand up in it, I could grope round and touch the slippery walls of its insides, and I thanked God for saving me from drowning. 'All your waves billowed over me,' I cried. 'I thought you would never see me again. My life was ebbing away. But I did not forget you, Lord.'

Soon I was wrapped round with strands of seaweed that had slid into the monster fish's mouth at the same time as me, and the reeds wrapped themselves round me like a burial shroud. I lay there, quite still, quite calm, for three days, until the fish opened its mouth and spewed me out again onto land.

I stood up slowly and shook myself like a dog. I could hardly believe I was alive.

And God said: *Now go to Nineveh, Jonah.*

I groaned inside, but this time I knew I couldn't escape. 'What do you want me to do there?' I asked.

You must tell the people there that in forty days their city will be destroyed.

I was not happy about going to that place of infidels and outlaws to give them news like this, but I did as I was told. The city was so huge that it took me three days to walk from one side to the other, and wherever I went I shouted out, 'Forty days from now, and your city will be destroyed. Thirty-nine days from now, and your city will be destroyed. Thirty-eight days from now, and your city will be destroyed.' And so on.

The people looked at me as if I was mad. Maybe I did look strange; I had just spent three days wrapped up in seaweed inside the belly of a monster fish, after all. But instead of chasing me and jeering at me and waving knives at me as I expected, they took me to their king, and in great fear I gave him the same message. He didn't throw me to the lions or cast me down a pit of snakes. He removed his royal garments and dressed himself in sackcloth; he smeared his face with ashes, and he ordered everyone to do the same thing.

'Wear the clothes of mourning,' he said. 'Our city is about to die, and we will die with it. We must all fast, men, women, children, and animals. Cry to God to forgive us.'

When the forty days were up I left the city and went and sat up on a hillside to see what would happen. Would Nineveh go up in flames, or disappear in a crack in the earth, or be crushed by rocks, or be washed away in a flood? Whatever happened, it would be a magnificent spectacle, and I wanted to be sure to see it. From where I was sitting I could see the city wall, eight miles long. I could see the fine buildings and parks, the sparkling pools, the glowing flower gardens. I waited and waited, and nothing happened.

I was really angry. I had left Tarshish, I had suffered the torture of seasickness, I had given myself to be drowned, I had lived in the belly of a monster fish, I had risked having my throat cut by the rogues of Nineveh, and all for nothing!

I waited another day, and the sun burned down on me, and kind God planted a tree that grew over me and sheltered me from the sun. I fell asleep in its shade, and during the night an invisible worm ate the roots of the tree and it perished. I couldn't believe that this could happen, that God could plant a tree for me and then just let it die.

I wanted to die then. I was angry and ashamed, the sun beat down on me and I was sick with fever.

'Let me die, Lord, let me die,' I begged him. 'I'd rather die than live. Why did you give me a tree and let it perish?'

You are very angry.
Why are you angry about the death of a tree?
Did you plant it, or feed it, or water it?
It is no concern of yours.

And why should I be concerned about Nineveh?

Yet I am.

This is a great city,

and these are my people,

just as you are.

I gave them life,

I gave them food and water.

They do not know right from wrong,

they do not know I am their true God,

but I have spared them.

That is what I learned when I went to Nineveh. God is a gracious God, he is merciful, he is slow to anger and willing to forgive. He is the same God who flooded Noah's world and who brought plagues on the people of Egypt, who gave Sarah a son when she was a hundred years old, who accepted Jephtha's daughter as a sacrifice.

I don't understand him, and he does not ask me to understand him.

And now I go back to Galilee, back to my people, and, if God is willing, I will live in peace for the rest of my days.

Index of People and Places

A

Aaron 89–90, 93, 97–100, 102, 111, 113, 116–118

Abednego (new name given to Azariah) 231–233

Abel 21–25

Abraham (name by which Abram was latterly known)
    47–49, 51–54, 62, 88, 93, 95, 119, 207–208, 213, 235

Abram 37–40, 42, 44–47

Absolom 188–190

Adam 14–16, 18–27

Adonijah 191–192

Ahab, King 202–203, 205–206, 213–214, 225

Ahaziah 225–226

Amittai 255

Ammeil 115

Ammonites 130–131, 254

Arabia 76

Arabs 254

Ararat 32

Artaxerxes, King 253

Ashdodites 254

Asher 66, 87, 115

Assyria 255

Azariah 228, 230–231

B

Baal 126, 202, 205–208

Babel, Tower of 34

Babylon 34, 230–232, 234, 242

Babylonians 253

Balshazzar 231, 234–237

Bathsheba 185–187

Belteshazzar (new name given to Daniel) 231

Benjamin 74–75, 83–87, 115

Bethlehem 146–148, 150, 152–153, 161–164

Bethuel 54

Bezalel 114

Bigthan 246, 249

Bilhah 66

Boaz 148–154

C

Cain 21–26

Caleb 115–117

Canaan 54, 64, 70, 81–82, 84, 87, 115–116,
    118, 120, 130–131, 137, 139

Carmel, Mount 206

Chilion 146–147

Cyrus, King 253

D

Dagon 143, 157

Damascus 213

Dan 66, 87, 115

Daniel 228–239, 242

Darius 238–239, 242

David (see also King David) 154, 161–165,
    167–176, 178–179

David, King (see also David) 180–191, 197, 201, 228, 253

Dead Sea 43, 147

Delilah 140–142

Dinah 66

E

Eden, Garden of 14–15, 18

Edom 70, 219

Egypt 38, 40, 76–77, 79–81, 83–85, 87–89, 92,
    94–99, 101–104, 108–110, 116–119, 203, 260

Egyptians 78, 88–89, 97, 99–105, 111, 117

Eli 155–157

Elijah 202–216, 220

Elimelech 146–147, 149, 152–153

Elisha 213–216, 218–223, 225–227

Endor 177

Ephraim 115

Esau 55–60, 62–63, 69–73

Esther 244–246, 248, 251–252

Ethiopia 243

Euphrates, River 230, 233

Eve 14–16 18–23, 25–27

G

Gad 66, 76, 87, 115

Gaddi 115–116

Gaddiel 115–116

Galilee 255, 260

Garden of Eden 14–15, 18, 20

Gaza 140, 143

Gehazi 221, 223–224

Geuel 115

Gibeon 192–193

Gideon 125–129

Gilboa, Mount 176, 178

Gilead 68, 225

Gilgal 123

Goliath 164–165, 167–168

Gomorrah 40–43

Goshen 88–89, 104

Great Sea 137

H

Hagar 46–47, 49–50

Ham 28–29

Haman 244, 246–252

Hananiah 228, 230–231

Hannah 155

Haran 37–38, 60, 63

Hazael, King 213

Hebrews 88–89, 97, 100, 102, 165, 167, 252

Hebron 180

Hiram of Tyre, King 197

Hor, Mount 118

Horeb, Mount 111, 211

I

Igal 115

India 243

Isaac 49, 51–55, 57–60, 62, 93, 95, 119, 207–208, 213, 235

Isaachar 66, 87, 115

Ishmael 47–50

Israel (name by which Jacob was latterly known) 72, 88

Israel (nation) 104, 109, 113, 125, 157–160, 176,
     178, 180, 184, 191, 199, 201–203, 205–209, 210,
     212–214, 216–217, 219–222, 225–226, 228

Israelites 88–89, 102, 104–105, 108, 112, 114–125,
     130–131, 134, 139, 143, 157–159, 161, 165, 168,
     175, 179–182, 197, 201, 203, 217, 219

J

Jabbok 72

Jacob 55–60, 62–74, 77, 83–84, 87–88, 93, 95, 115,
     119, 122, 199, 253

Japheth 28–29

Jebusites 180

Jehoshaphat 225

Jehu, King 213, 225–228

Jephtha 130–135

Jephtha's daughter 130–135, 260

Jeraboam, King 200–201, 228

Jericho 119–120, 122–124, 214, 216

Jerusalem 180–181, 186, 188–189, 201, 228–231,
     236, 239, 253–254

Jesse 161–162

Jesus of Nazareth 154

Jethro 109

Jews 228, 231, 243, 247, 249, 252–255

Jezebel 202–203, 205–207, 210, 213, 225–226

Jezreel 226

Joab 186, 188–189

Jonah 255, 258

Jonathan 163, 168–169, 172–174, 176, 178–179

Joppa 255

Joram, King 225–226

Jordan, River 120, 123, 126, 221–222

Joseph 66, 74–87, 104, 115

Joshua 115, 117, 120–123, 125

Judah (district) 137, 180, 201, 219, 226, 228–229, 232

Judah (son of Jacob) 66, 76, 83–87, 115

K

King Ahab 202–203, 205–206, 213–214, 225

King Artaxerxes 253

King Cyrus 253

King David (see also David) 180–191, 197, 201, 228, 253

King Hazael 213

King Hiram of Tyre 197

King Jehu 213, 225–228

King Jeraboam 200–201, 228

King Joram 225–226

King Nebuchadnezzar 228–236, 253

King Rehoboam 200–201

King Saul (see also Saul) 160–161, 163–165, 167–180, 183, 189

King Solomon 191–197, 199–200, 228, 230, 236, 239

King Xerxes 243–247, 249, 251–252

L

Laban 60, 63–69

Leah 64–66, 70, 72

Lebanon 197

Levi 66, 87

Lot 37–38, 40–44

Lot's wife 38, 40–43

M

Mahlon 146–147

Mamre 44, 48

Merab 163, 171

Meshach (new name given to Mishael) 231–233

Mesopotamia 54

Michal 163, 171–174, 182, 186

Midian 109

Midianites 125–130

Miriam 89–90, 92–93, 108, 118

Mishael 228, 230–231

Moab 146, 148, 153, 219

Mordecai 244–246, 248–250, 252

Moses 92–102, 104–105, 108–120, 199, 235

Mount Ararat 32

Mount Carmel 206

Mount Gilboa 176, 178

Mount Hor 118

Mount Horeb 111, 211

Mount Nebo 118–119

Mount Sinai 94, 110–111, 113, 199

Mount Sodom 43

N

Nahbi 115

Nahor 54

Namaan 217–224

Naomi 146–148, 150–154

Naphthali 66, 87, 115

Nathan 183, 186–187

Nazareth 154

Nebo, Mount 118–119

Nebuchadnezzar, King 228–236, 253

Nehemiah 253–254

Nile, River 38, 80–81, 89–90, 99

Ninevah 255, 258–260

Noah 27–34, 37, 260

O

Obed 154

Orpah 146–147

P

Palti 115–116

Persia 243–245, 247–248, 252–253

Pharaoh Rameses the second 88–89

Philistines 137, 139–143, 157–158, 160, 164–165,
    168, 170–171, 175–176, 178–180

Potiphar 77–78

Promised Land, the 95, 98, 110, 114, 119, 122, 125

R

Rachel 63–66, 68–70, 72, 74–75

Rahab 121–122, 124

Rameses the second, Pharaoh 88–89

Rebeka 54–55, 57–58, 60

Red Sea 88, 101, 104, 122

Rehoboam, King 200–201

Reuben 66, 76–77, 82, 84–85, 87, 115

River Euphrates 230, 233

River Jordan 120, 123, 126, 221–222

River Nile 38, 80–81, 89–90, 99

Ruth 146–154

S

Samaria 220

Samson 136–143

Samuel 155–162, 168–169, 175–178

Sarah (name by which Sarai was latterly known)
    47–49, 51, 260

Sarai 37–40, 44, 46–47

Saul 158–159

Saul, King (see also Saul) 160–161, 163–165,
    167–180, 183, 189

Semites 37

Sethur 115

Shadrach (new name given to Hananiah) 231–233

Shammua 115–116

Shaphar 115–116

Shem 28–29, 37

Shiloh 155, 157

Sidonians 197

Simeon 66, 74, 76, 83–85, 87, 115

Sinai, Mount 94, 110–111, 113, 199

Sodom 40–43

Sodom, Mount 43

Solomon, King 191–197, 199–200, 228, 230, 236, 239

Susa 243, 246–247, 250, 252

Syria 213, 219–221, 223, 228

Syrians 220

T

Tarshish 255, 259

Teresh 246, 249

Timnah 138–139

Tower of Babel 34

U

Uriah (the Hittite) 185–186

V

Vashti 243, 244

X

Xerxes, King 243–247, 249, 251–252

Z

Zaphenath-Paneah 82, 84, 86

Zarephath 203–204

Zebulun 66, 87, 115

Zilpah 66